RUNAWAYS

ESCAPE TO
NEW YORK

RUNAWAYS

WRITER **BRIAN K. VAUGHAN**
PENCILS **TAKESHI MIYAZAWA** (ISSUES #7-8)
ADRIAN ALPHONA (ISSUES #9-12)
INKER **CRAIG YEUNG**
COLORIST CHRISTINA STRAIN ARTIST, X-MEN/RUNAWAYS SKOTTIE YOUNG
LETTERER VIRTUAL CALLIGRAPHY'S RANDY GENTILE
COVER ART CHRIS BACHALO, JO CHEN & JAMES JEAN
ASSISTANT EDITOR NATHAN COSBY EDITOR MACKENZIE CADENHEAD
SPECIAL THANKS TO C.B. CEBULSKI
RUNAWAYS CREATED BY BRIAN K. VAUGHAN & ADRIAN ALPHONA

Collection Editor: Jennifer Grünwald
Editorial Assistants: James Emmett & Joe Hochstein
Assistant Editors: Alex Starbuck & Nelson Ribeiro
Editor, Special Projects: Mark D. Beazley
Senior Editor, Special Projects: Jeff Youngquist
Vice President of Sales: David Gabriel
SVP of Brand Planning & Communications: Michael Pasciullo
Book Design: Jeff Powell

Editor in Chief: Axel Alonso
Chief Creative Officer: Joe Quesada
Publisher: Dan Buckley
Executive Producer: Alan Fine

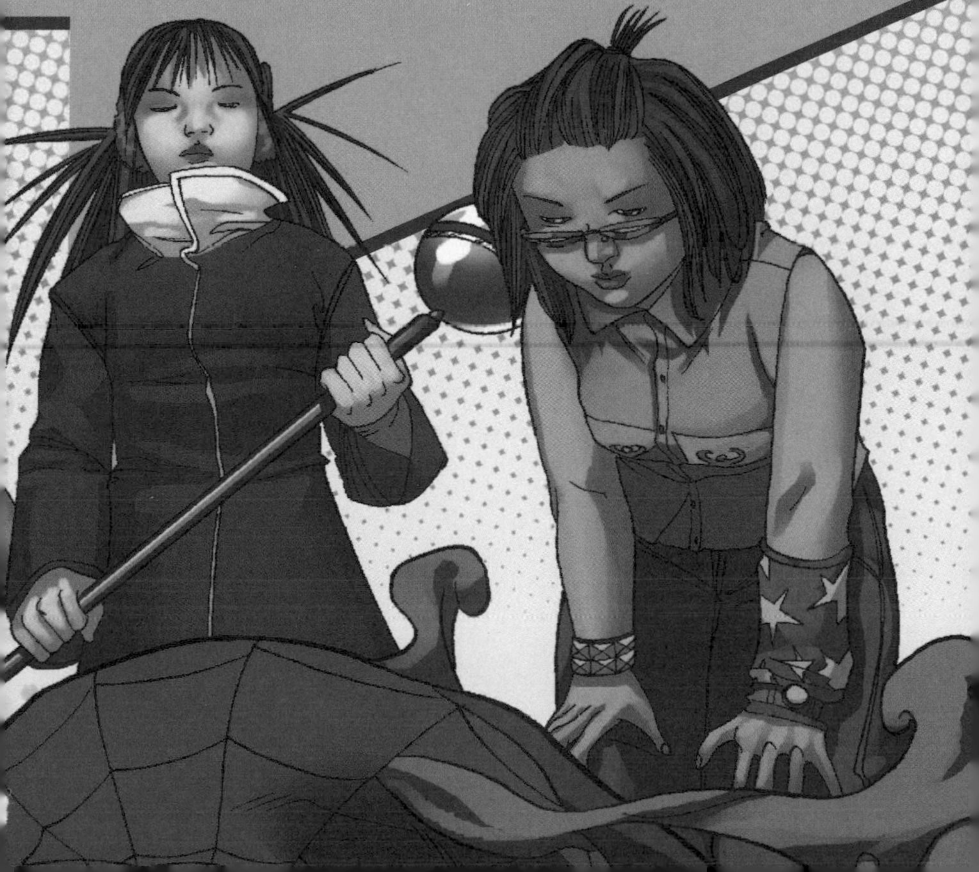

KAROLINA DEAN

VICTOR MANCHA

MOLLY HAYES

At some point in their lives, all kids think that they have the most evil parents in the world, but Karolina Dean and her friends really did.

Discovering that they were the children of a group of super villains known as The Pride, the teenagers stole weapons and resources from these criminals before running away from home and eventually defeating their parents. But that was just the beginning.

The young group's newest recruit is Victor Mancha, the half-robot/half-human son of an evil killing machine called Ultron. Together, Victor and his fellow runaways now hope to atone for their parents' crimes by taking on the new threats trying to fill The Pride's void.

NICO MINORU

GERTRUDE YORKES

CHASE STEIN

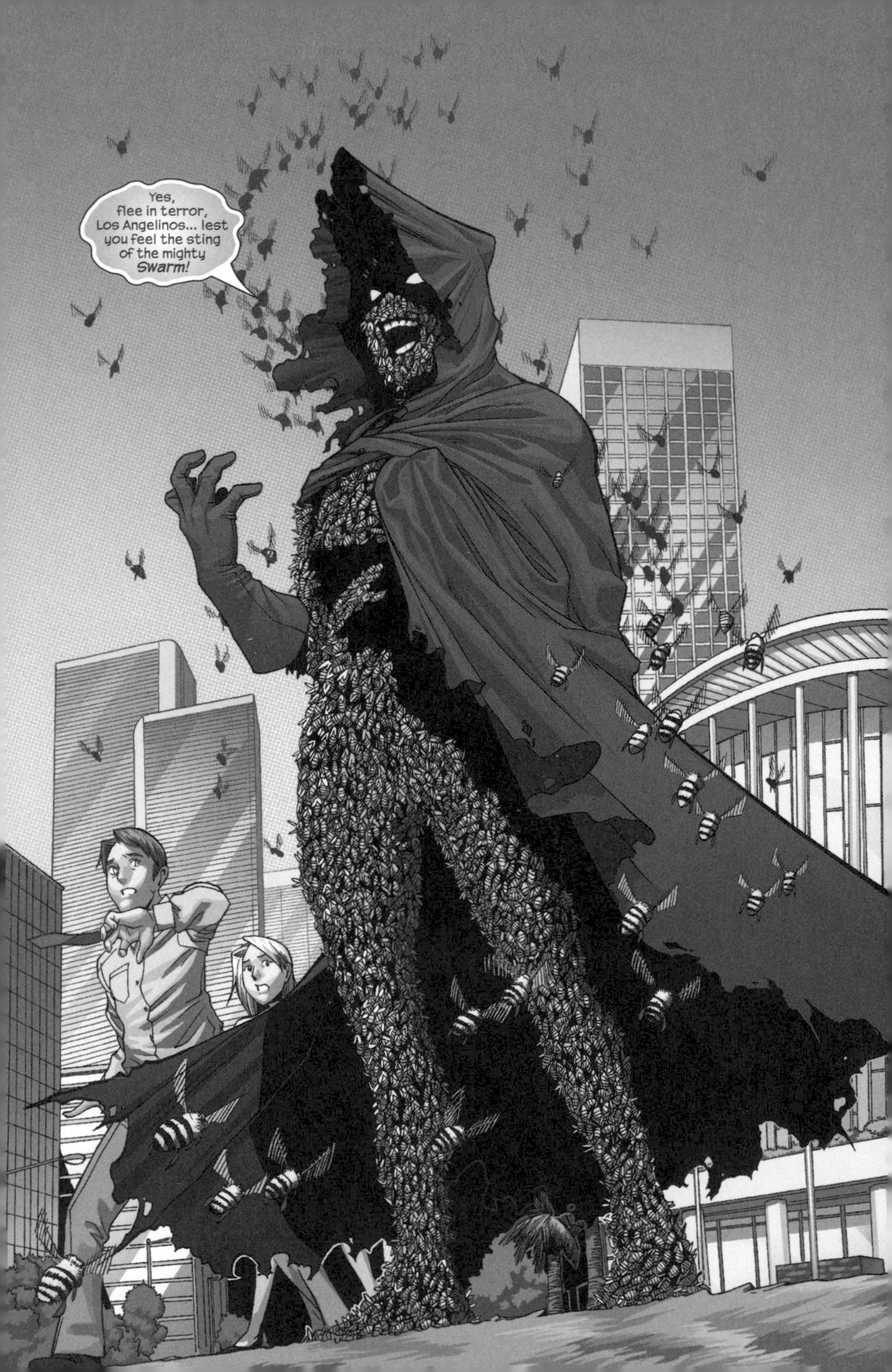
Yes, flee in terror, Los Angelinos... lest you feel the sting of the mighty Swarm!

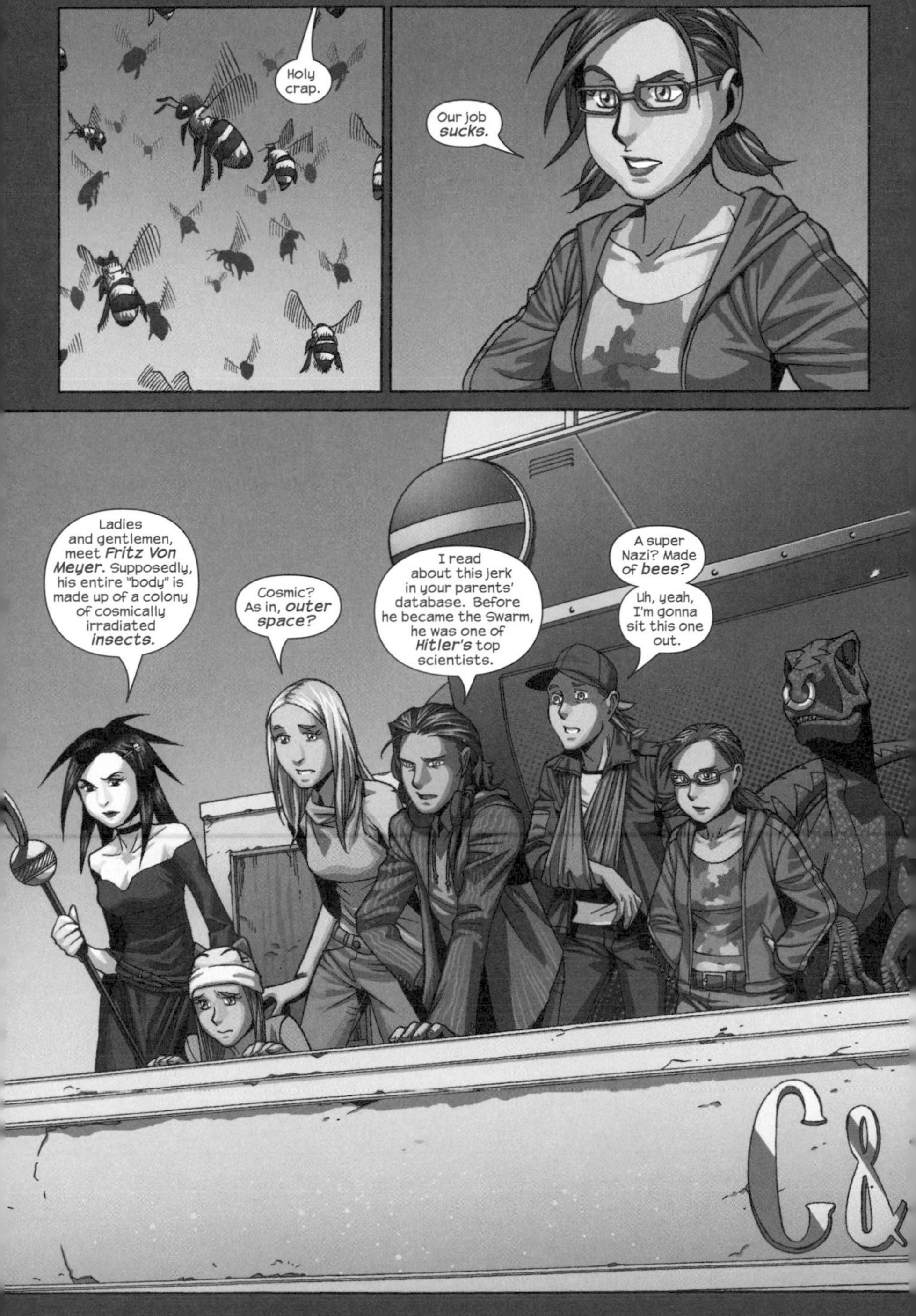

Holy crap.
Our job sucks.
Ladies and gentlemen, meet Fritz Von Meyer. Supposedly, his entire "body" is made up of a colony of cosmically irradiated insects.
Cosmic? As in, outer space?
I read about this jerk in your parents' database. Before he became the Swarm, he was one of Hitler's top scientists.
A super Nazi? Made of bees?
Uh, yeah, I'm gonna sit this one out.

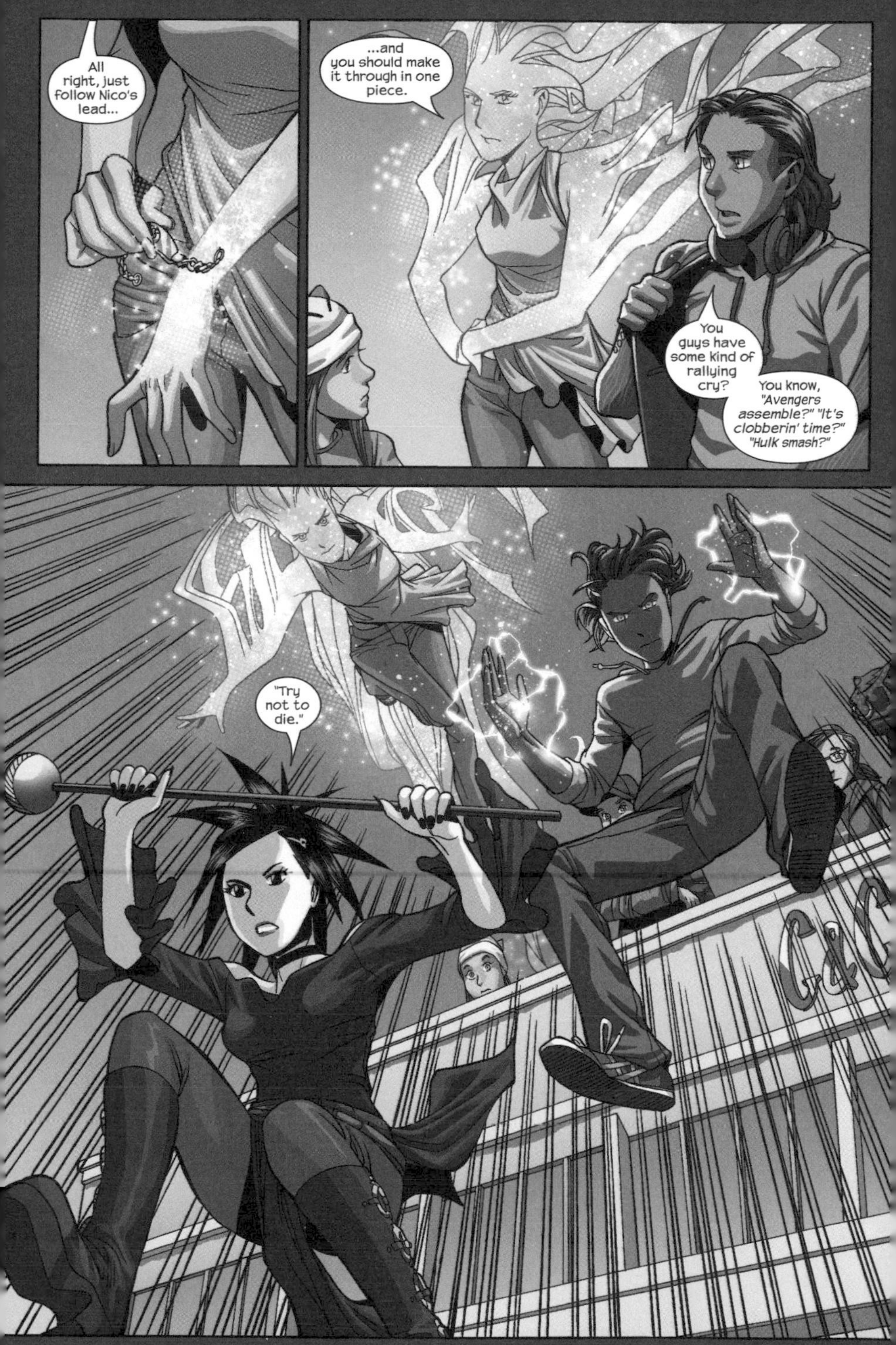
All right, just follow Nico's lead...
...and you should make it through in one piece.
You guys have some kind of rallying cry?
You know, "Avengers assemble?" "It's clobberin' time?" "Hulk smash?"
"Try not to die."

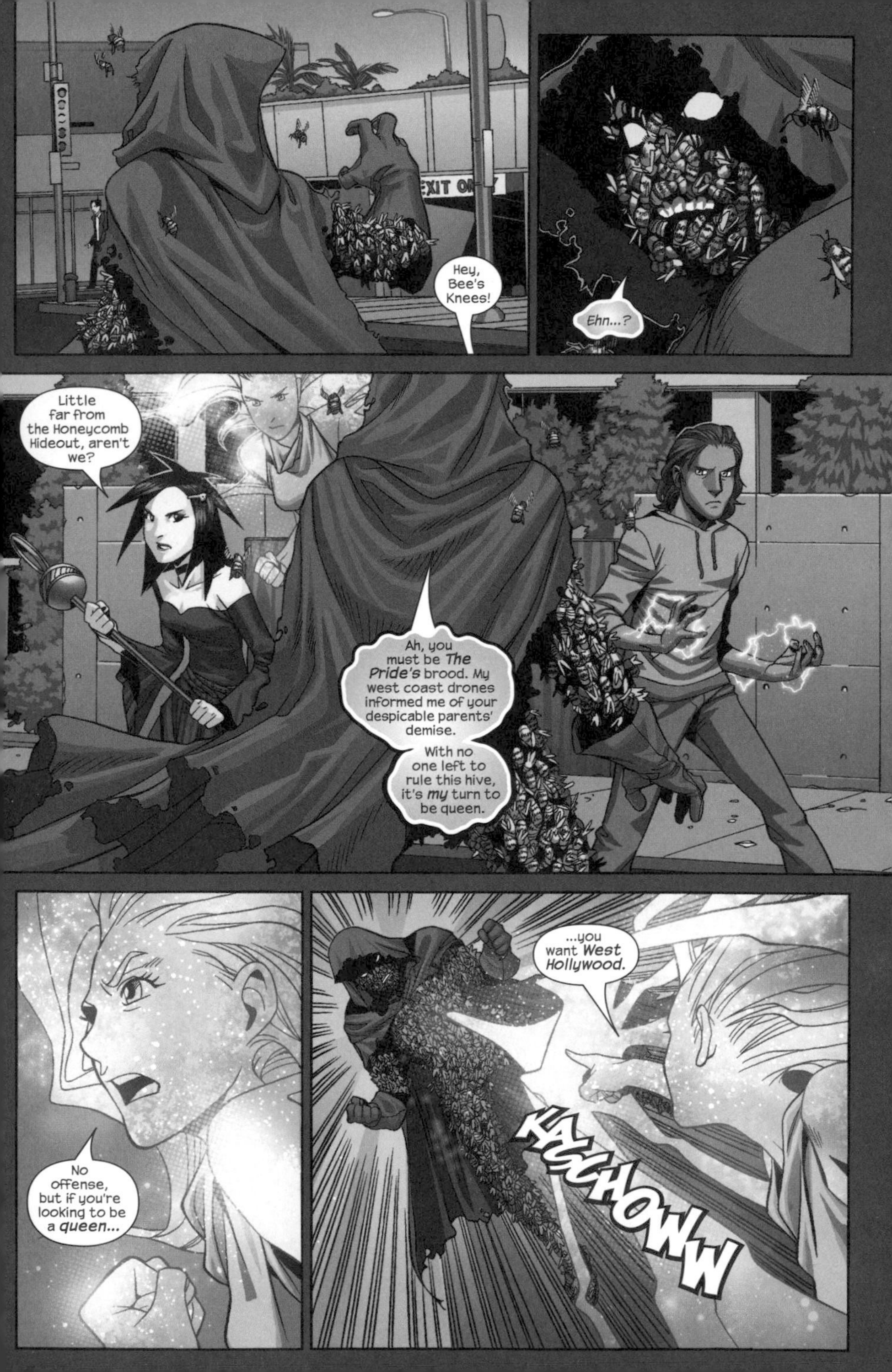
EXIT ONLY
Hey, Bee's Knees!
Ehn...?
Little far from the Honeycomb Hideout, aren't we?
Ah, you must be The Pride's brood. My west coast drones informed me of your despicable parents' demise.
With no one left to rule this hive, it's my turn to be queen.
No offense, but if you're looking to be a queen...
...you want West Hollywood.
KA-CHOWW

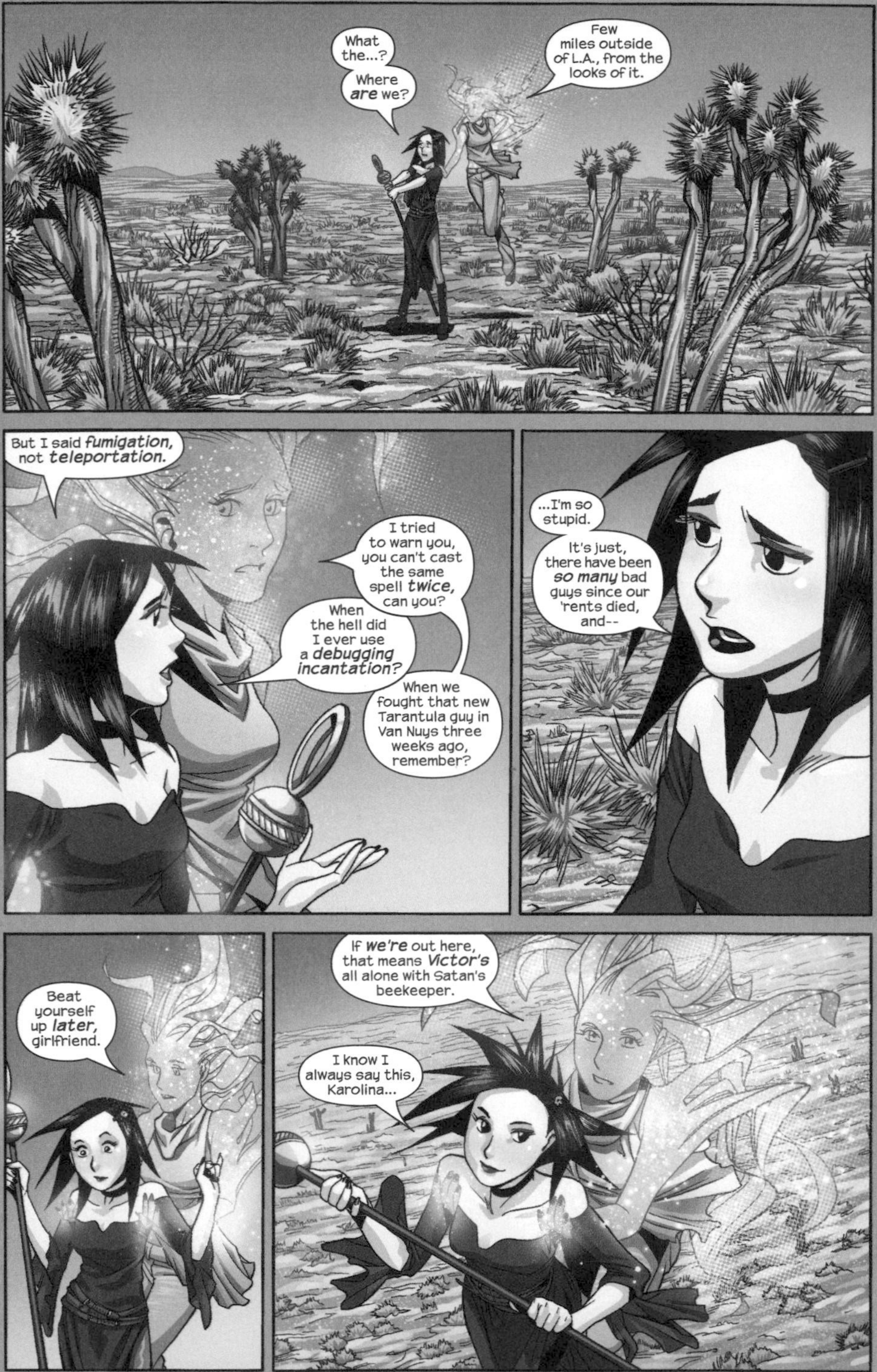
What the...?
Where *are* we?
Few miles outside of L.A., from the looks of it.
But I said *fumigation*, not *teleportation*.
I tried to warn you, you can't cast the same spell *twice*, can you?
When the hell did I ever use a *debugging incantation?*
When we fought that new Tarantula guy in Van Nuys three weeks ago, remember?
...I'm so stupid.
It's just, there have been *so many* bad guys since our 'rents died, and--
Beat yourself up *later*, girlfriend.
If *we're* out here, that means *Victor's* all alone with Satan's beekeeper.
I know I always say this, Karolina...

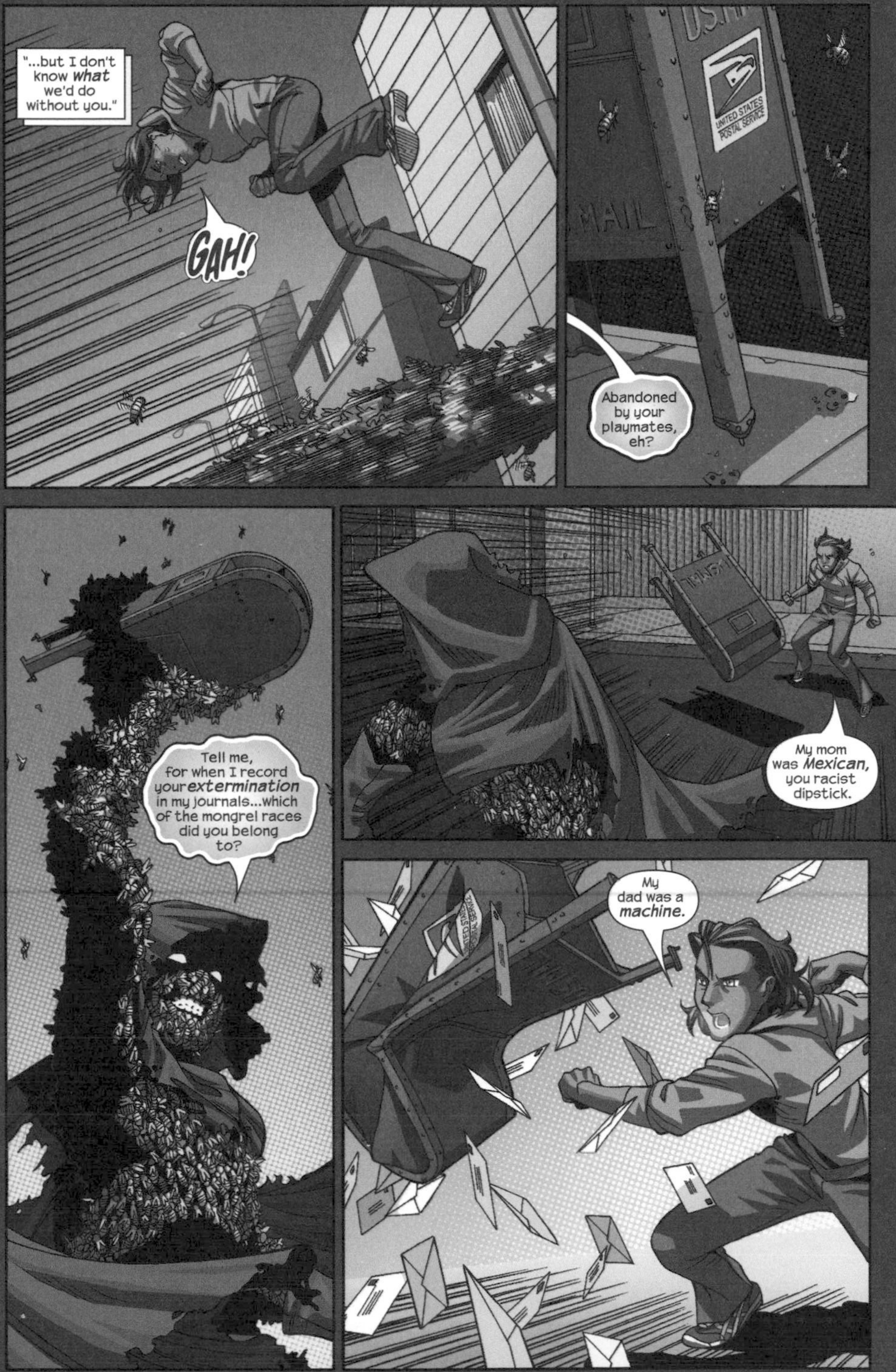
"...but I don't know *what* we'd do without you."
GAH!
D.S.M
UNITED STATES POSTAL SERVICE
MAIL
Abandoned by your playmates, eh?
Tell me, for when I record your *extermination* in my journals...which of the mongrel races did you belong to?
My mom was *Mexican,* you racist dipstick.
My dad was a *machine.*

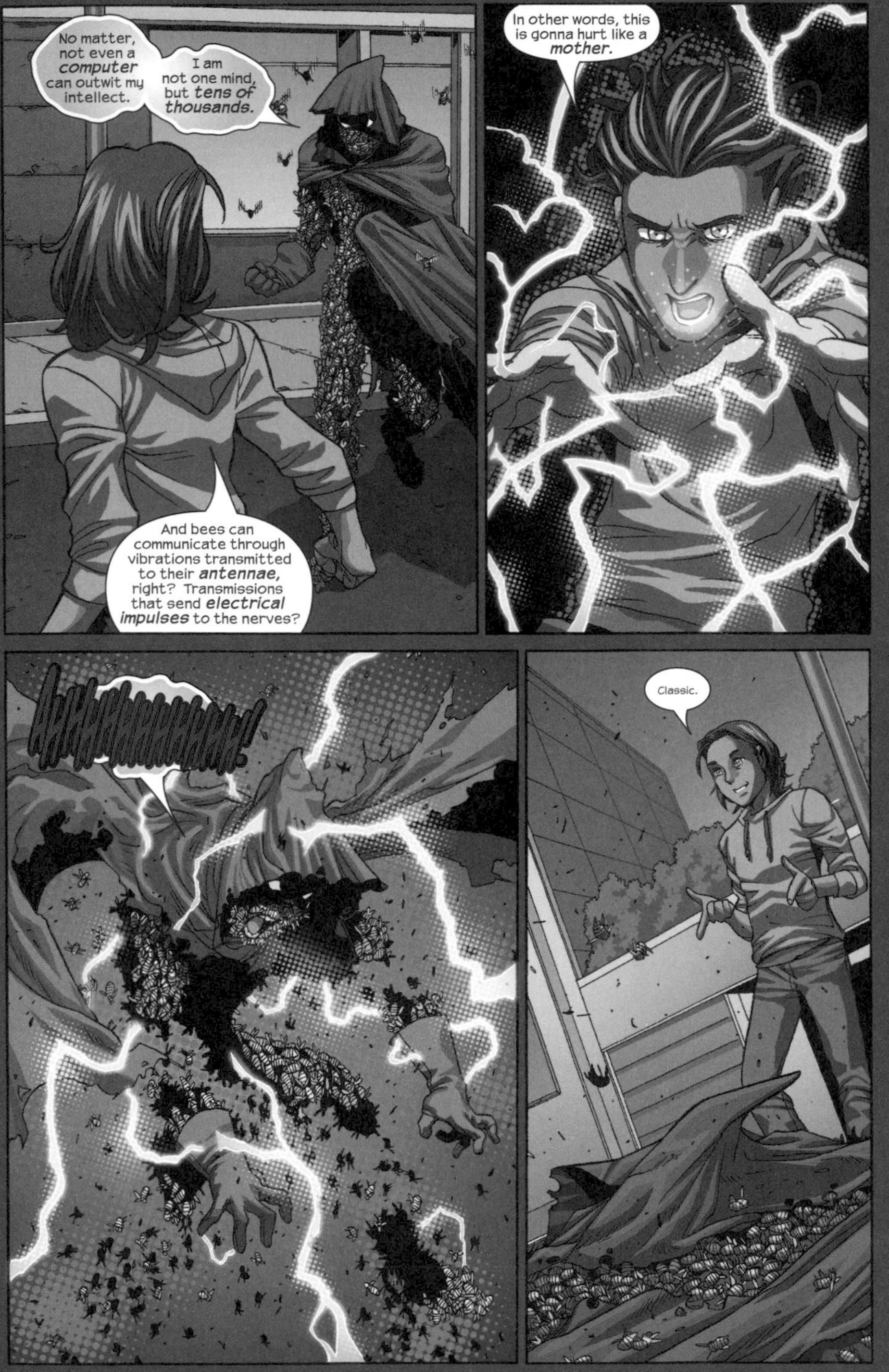
No matter, not even a computer can outwit my intellect.
I am not one mind, but tens of thousands.
And bees can communicate through vibrations transmitted to their antennae, right? Transmissions that send electrical impulses to the nerves?
In other words, this is gonna hurt like a mother.
AHHHHHHHHHHHH!
Classic.

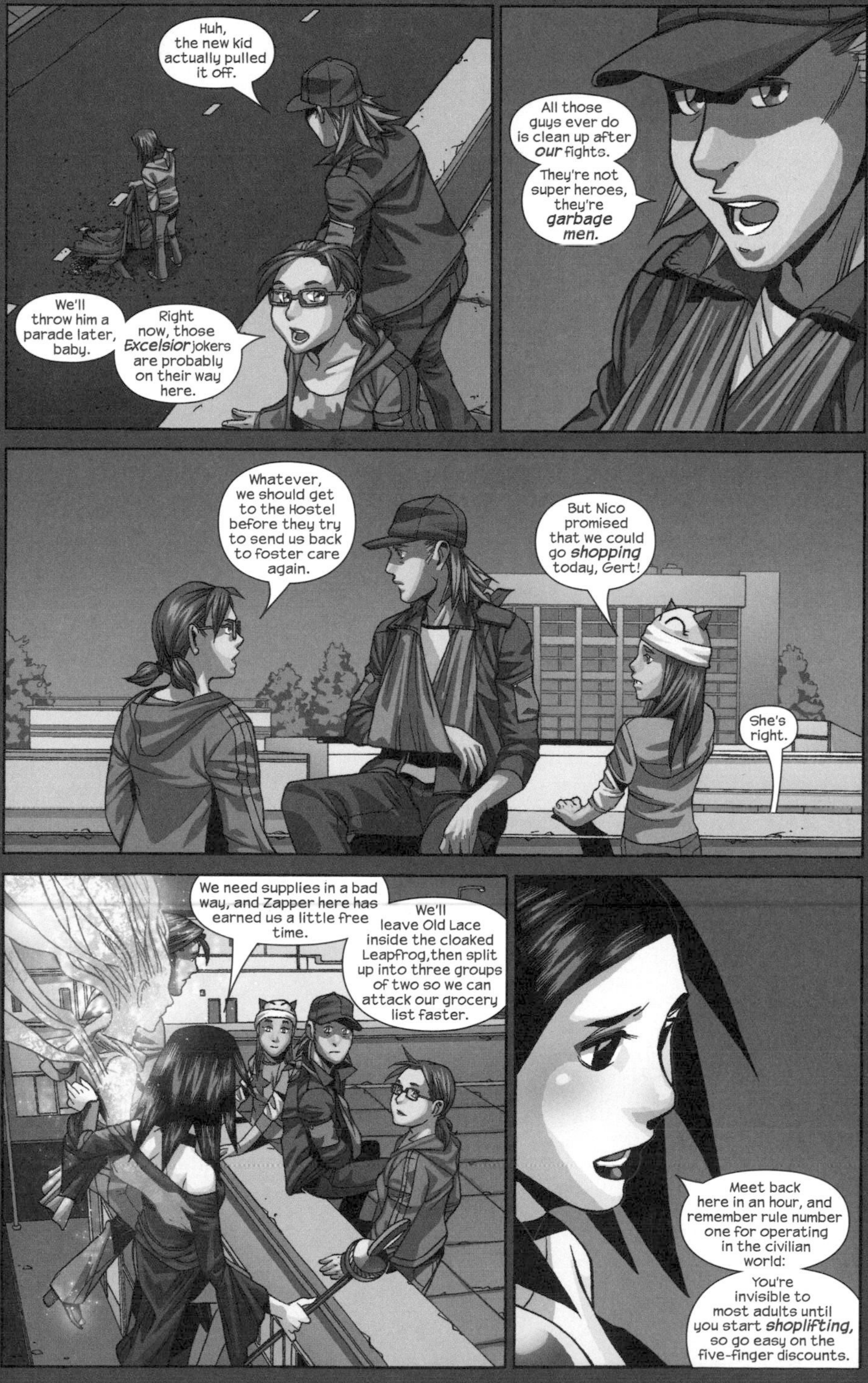
Huh, the new kid actually pulled it off.
All those guys ever do is clean up after our fights.
They're not super heroes, they're garbage men.
We'll throw him a parade later, baby.
Right now, those Excelsior jokers are probably on their way here.
Whatever, we should get to the Hostel before they try to send us back to foster care again.
But Nico promised that we could go shopping today, Gert!
She's right.
We need supplies in a bad way, and Zapper here has earned us a little free time.
We'll leave Old Lace inside the cloaked Leapfrog,then split up into three groups of two so we can attack our grocery list faster.
Meet back here in an hour, and remember rule number one for operating in the civilian world:
You're invisible to most adults until you start shoplifting, so go easy on the five-finger discounts.

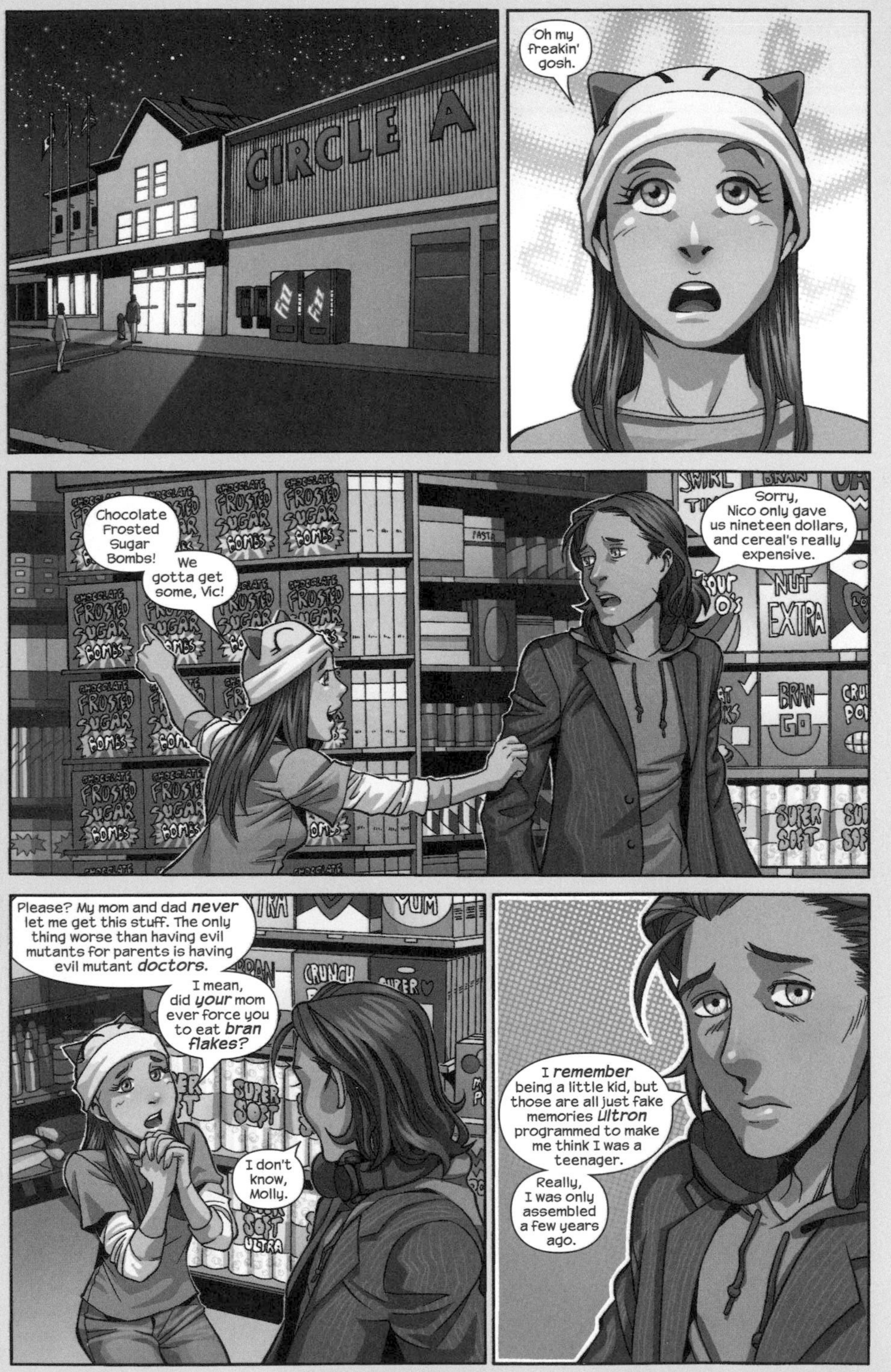

CIRCLE A
FIZZ
FIZZ
Oh my freakin' gosh.
Chocolate Frosted Sugar Bombs!
We gotta get some, Vic!
Sorry, Nico only gave us nineteen dollars, and cereal's really expensive.
Please? My mom and dad *never* let me get this stuff. The only thing worse than having evil mutants for parents is having evil mutant *doctors*.
I mean, did *your* mom ever force you to eat *bran flakes?*
I don't know, Molly.
I *remember* being a little kid, but those are all just fake memories *Ultron* programmed to make me think I was a teenager.
Really, I was only assembled a few years ago.

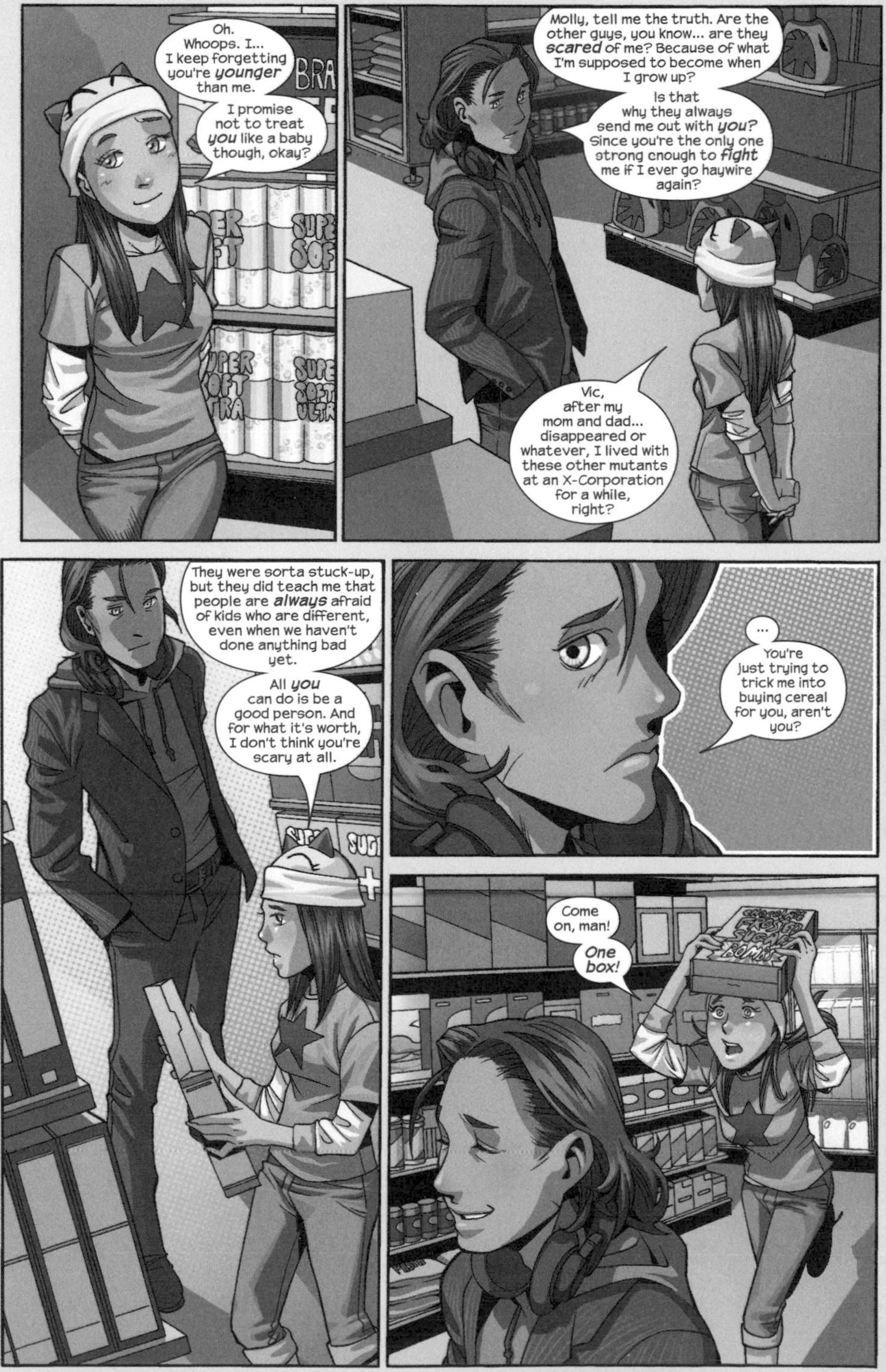
Oh. Whoops. I... I keep forgetting you're *younger* than me.
I promise not to treat *you* like a baby though, okay?
Molly, tell me the truth. Are the other guys, you know... are they *scared* of me? Because of what I'm supposed to become when I grow up?
Is that why they always send me out with *you?* Since you're the only one strong enough to *fight* me if I ever go haywire again?
Vic, after my mom and dad... disappeared or whatever, I lived with these other mutants at an X-Corporation for a while, right?
They were sorta stuck-up, but they did teach me that people are *always* afraid of kids who are different, even when we haven't done anything bad yet.
All *you* can do is be a good person. And for what it's worth, I don't think you're scary at all.
...
You're just trying to trick me into buying cereal for you, aren't you?
Come on, man!
One box!

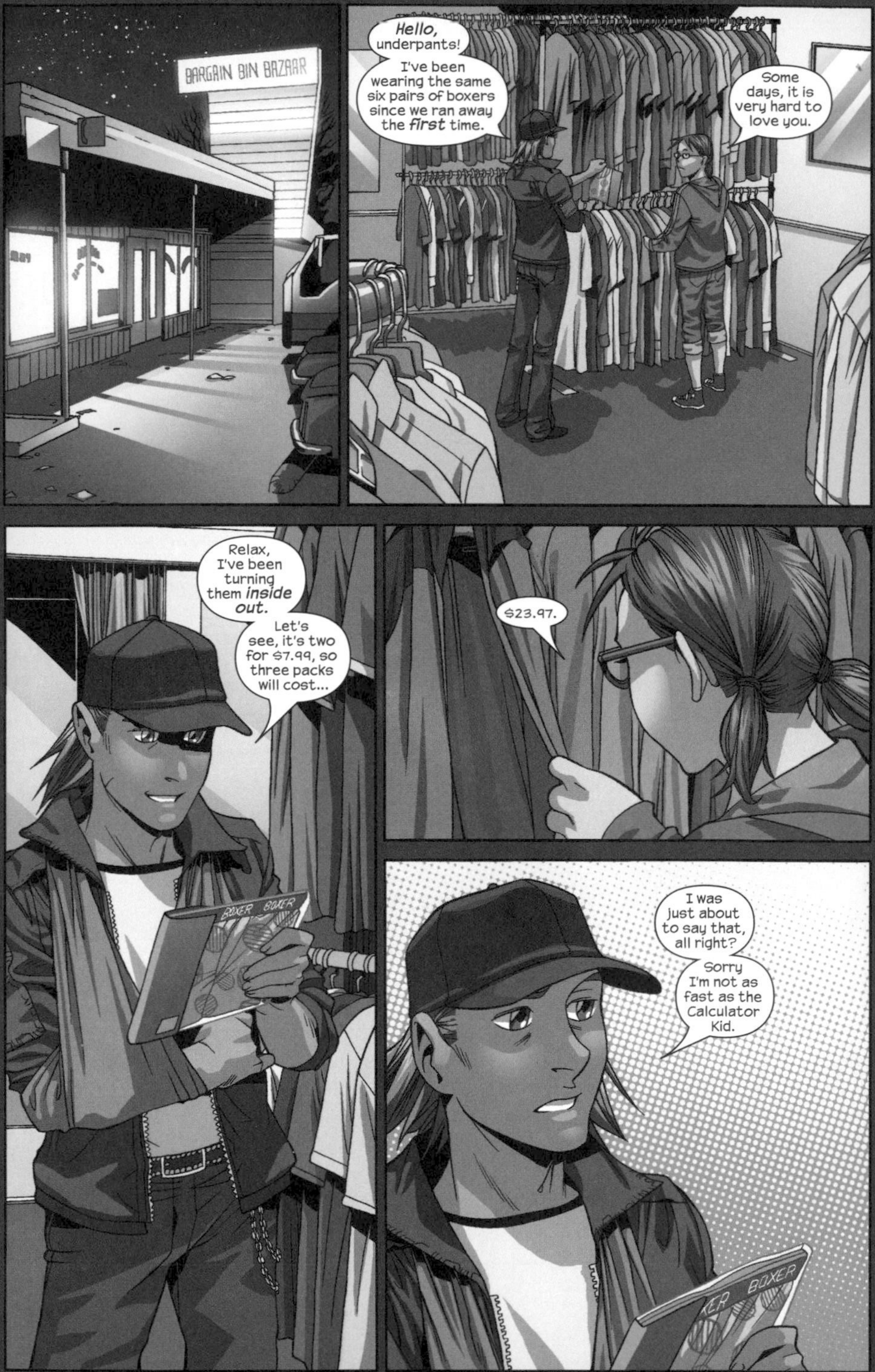
BARGAIN BIN BAZAAR
Hello, underpants!
I've been wearing the same six pairs of boxers since we ran away the *first* time.
Some days, it is very hard to love you.
Relax, I've been turning them *inside out.*
Let's see, it's two for $7.99, so three packs will cost...
$23.97.
BOXER BOXER
I was just about to say that, all right?
Sorry I'm not as fast as the Calculator Kid.

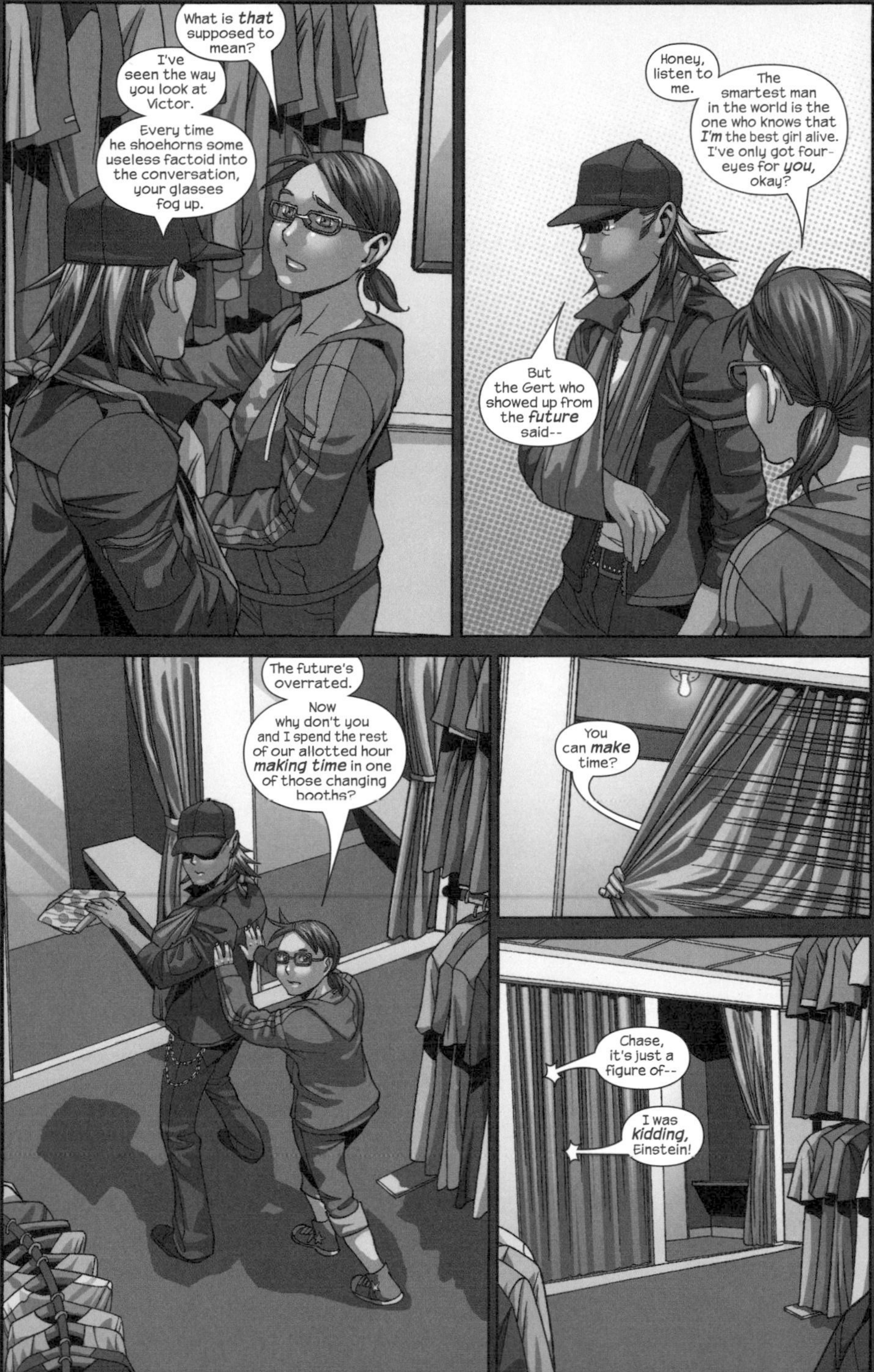
I've seen the way you look at Victor.
What is *that* supposed to mean?
Every time he shoehorns some useless factoid into the conversation, your glasses fog up.
Honey, listen to me.
The smartest man in the world is the one who knows that *I'm* the best girl alive. I've only got four-eyes for *you,* okay?
But the Gert who showed up from the *future* said--
The future's overrated.
Now why don't you and I spend the rest of our allotted hour *making time* in one of those changing booths?
You can *make* time?
Chase, it's just a figure of--
I was *kidding,* Einstein!

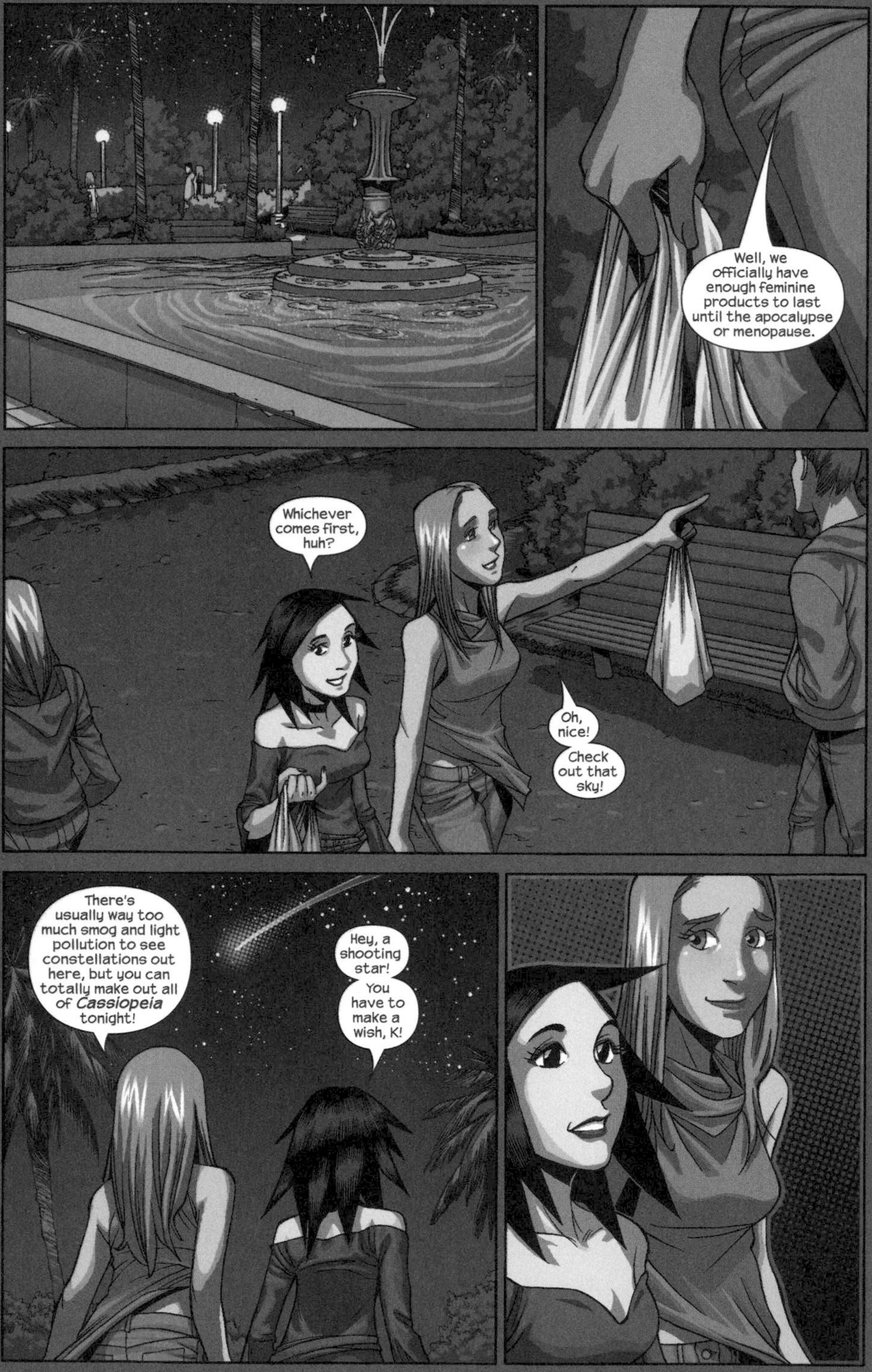
Well, we officially have enough feminine products to last until the apocalypse or menopause.
Whichever comes first, huh?
Oh, nice!
Check out that sky!
There's usually way too much smog and light pollution to see constellations out here, but you can totally make out all of *Cassiopeia* tonight!
Hey, a shooting star!
You have to make a wish, K!

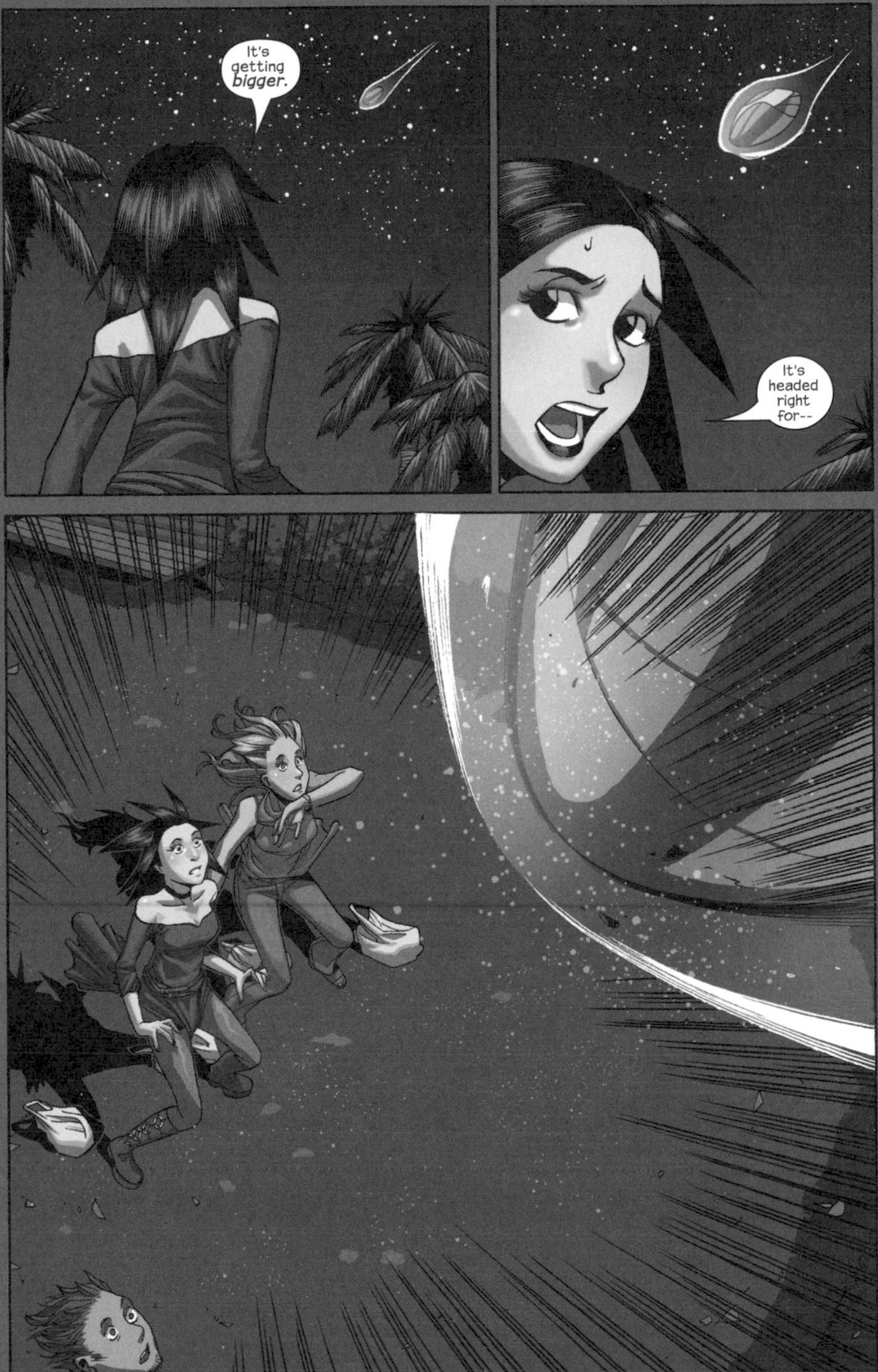
It's getting *bigger.*
It's headed right for--

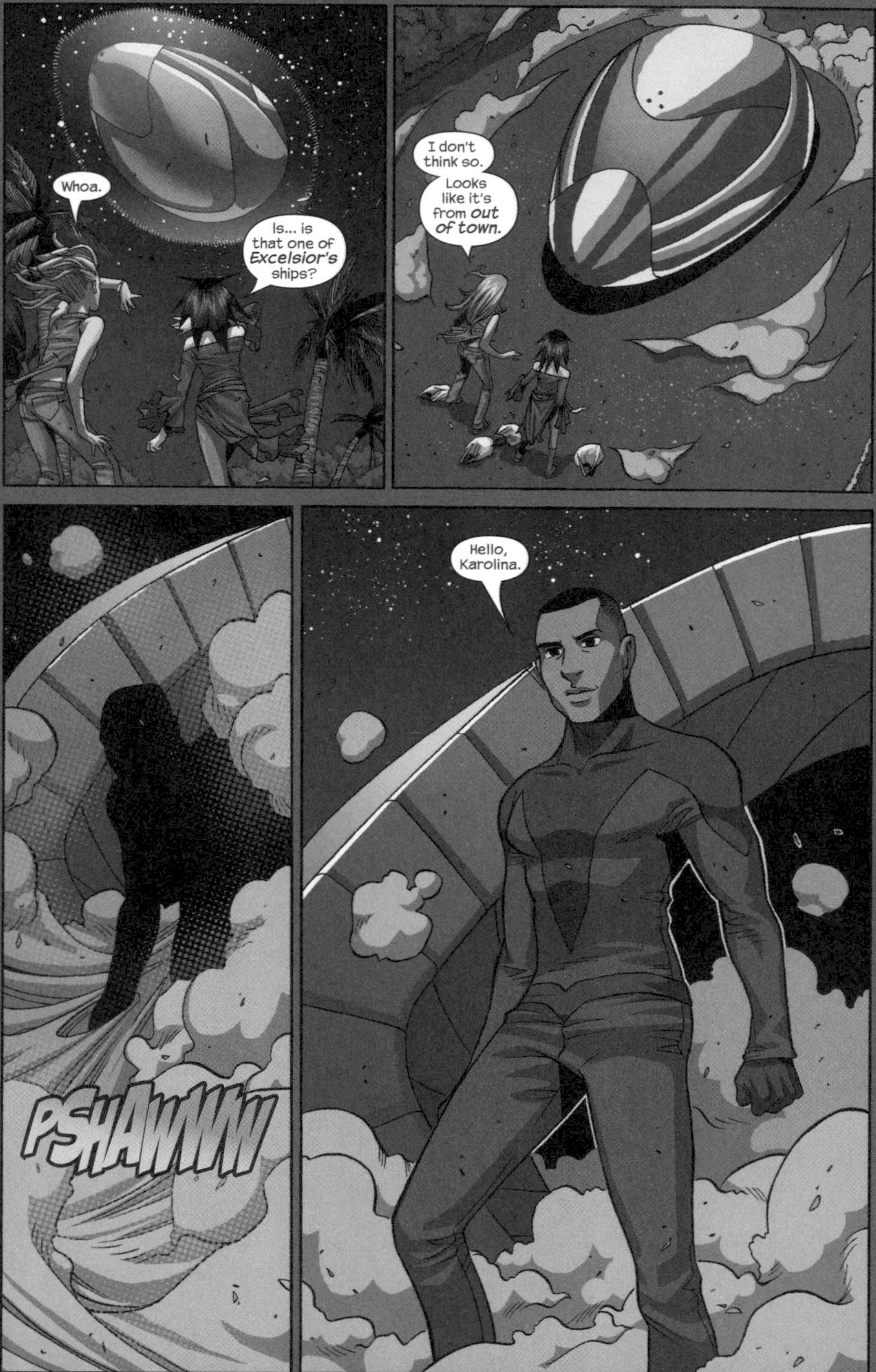
Whoa.
Is... is that one of Excelsior's ships?
I don't think so.
Looks like it's from out of town.
PSHAWWW
Hello, Karolina.

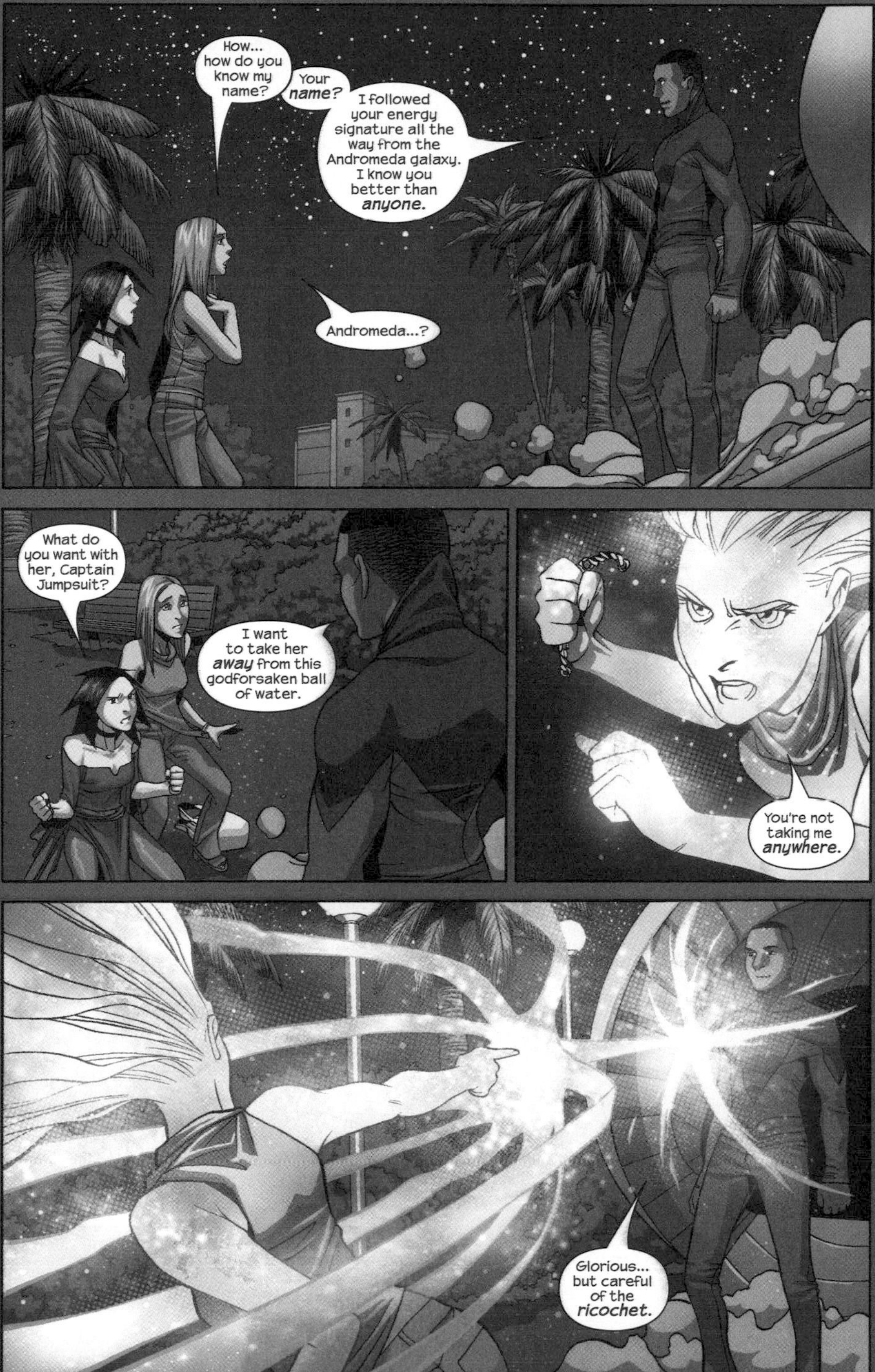
How... how do you know my name?
Your *name?*
I followed your energy signature all the way from the Andromeda galaxy. I know you better than *anyone.*
Andromeda...?
What do you want with her, Captain Jumpsuit?
I want to take her *away* from this godforsaken ball of water.
You're not taking me *anywhere.*
Glorious... but careful of the *ricochet.*

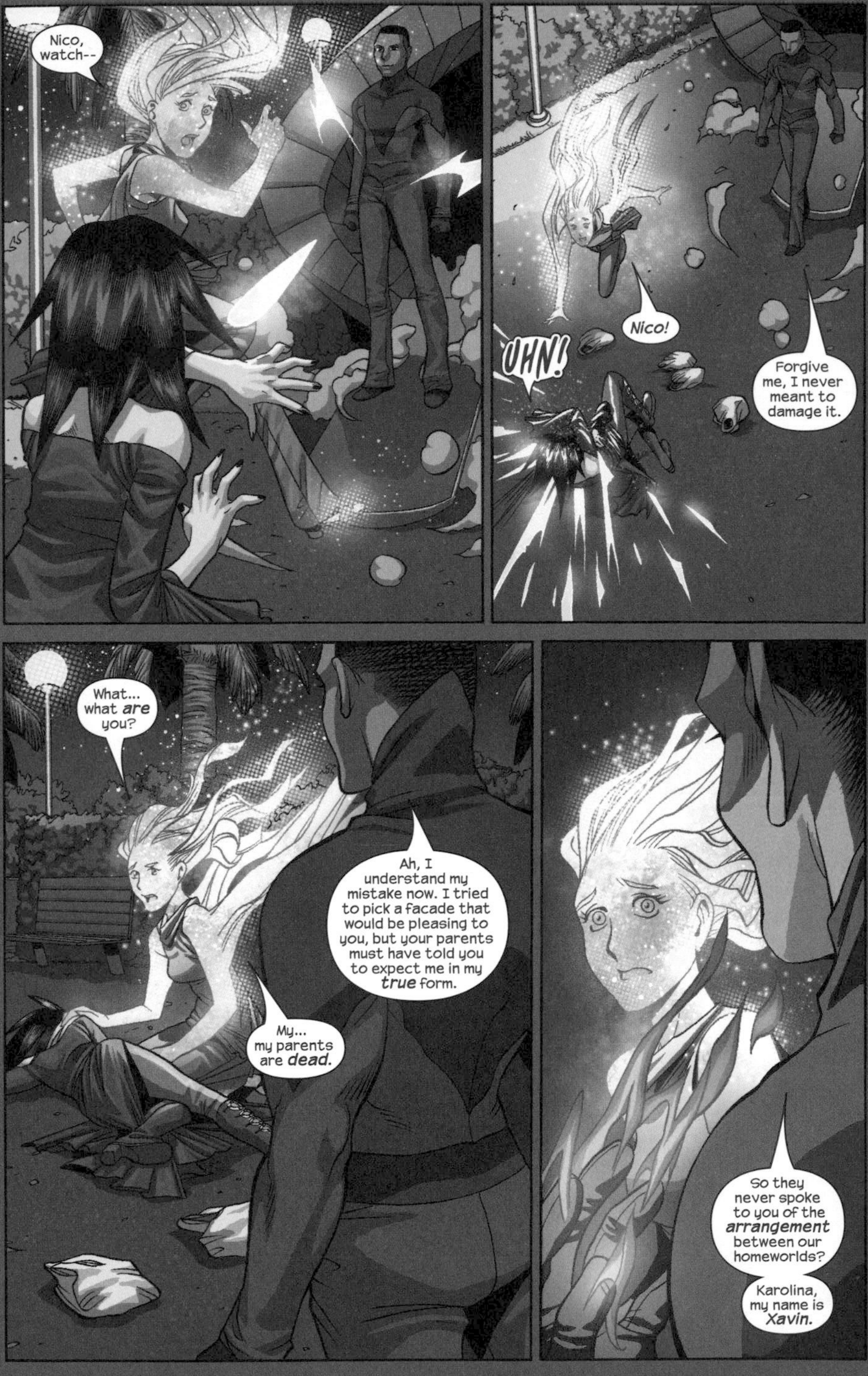
Nico, watch--
Nico!
UHN!
Forgive me, I never meant to damage it.
What... what *are* you?
Ah, I understand my mistake now. I tried to pick a facade that would be pleasing to you, but your parents must have told you to expect me in my *true* form.
My... my parents are *dead.*
So they never spoke to you of the *arrangement* between our homeworlds?
Karolina, my name is *Xavin.*

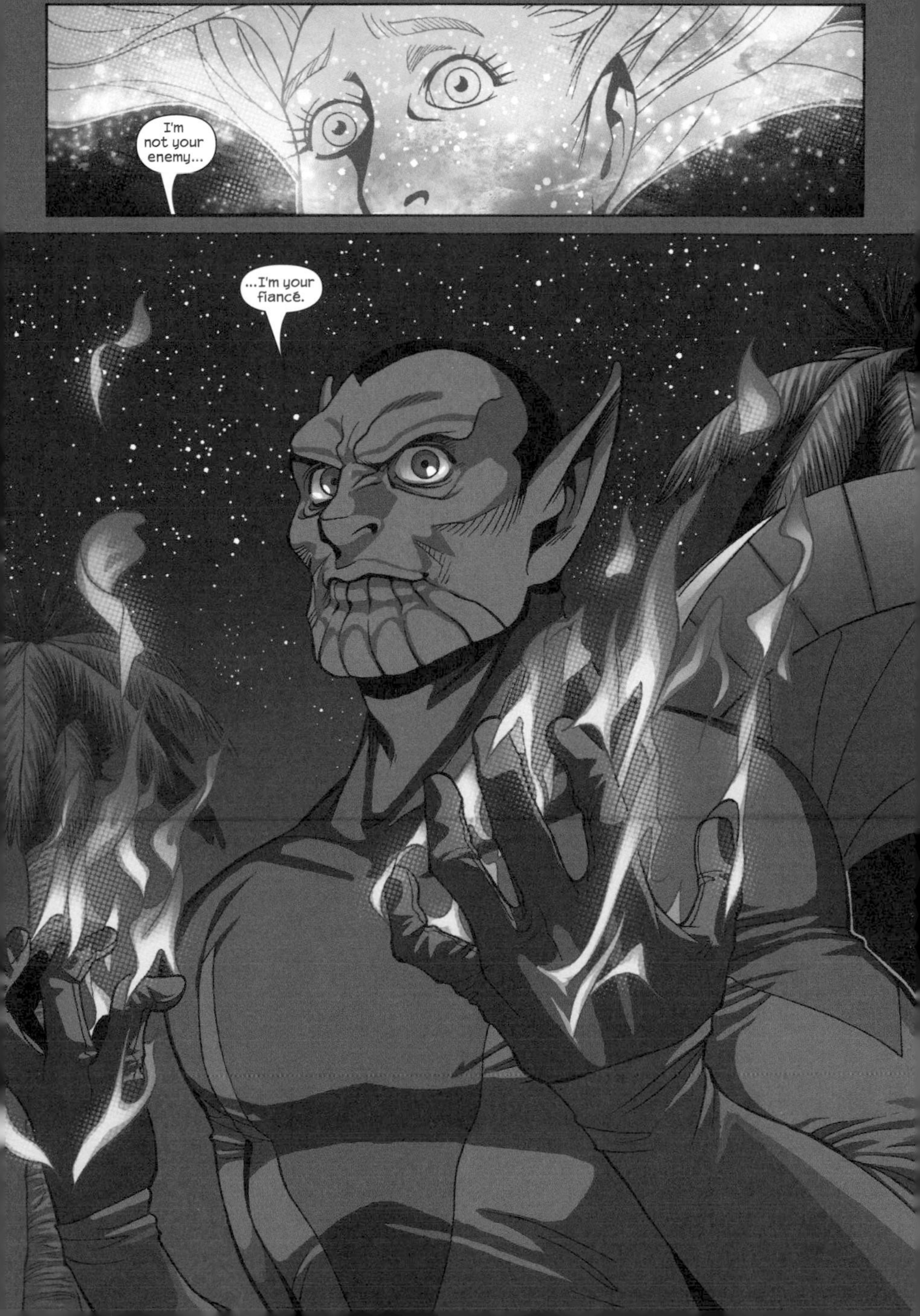
I'm not your enemy...
...I'm your fiancé.

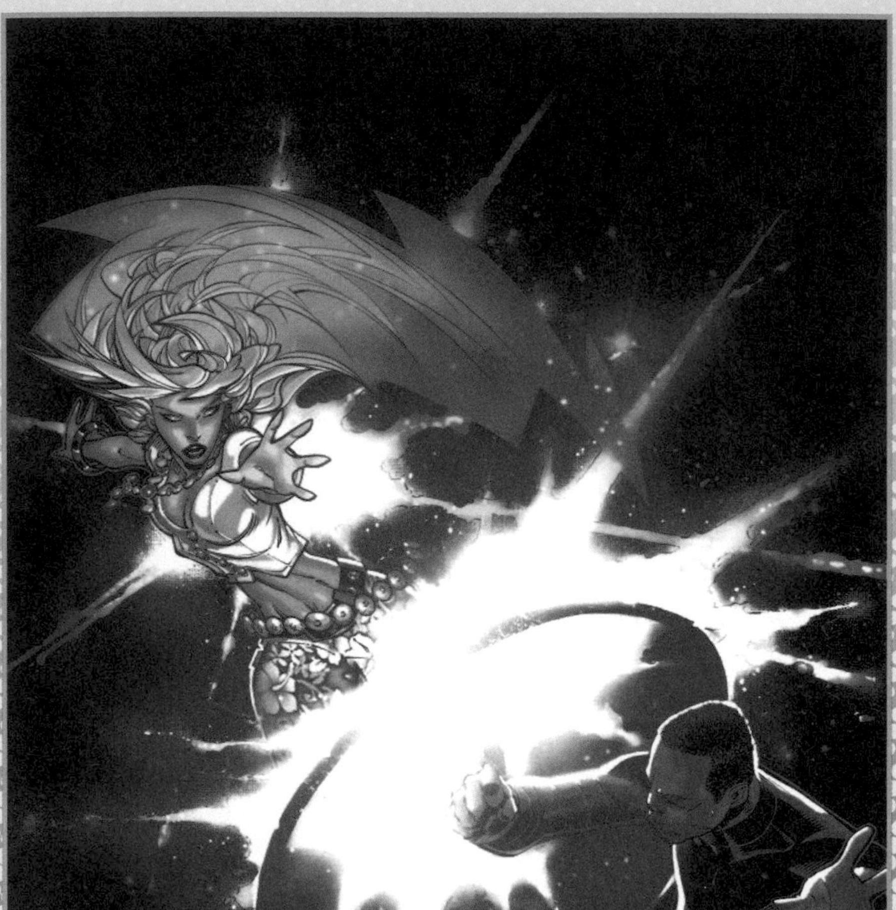

8

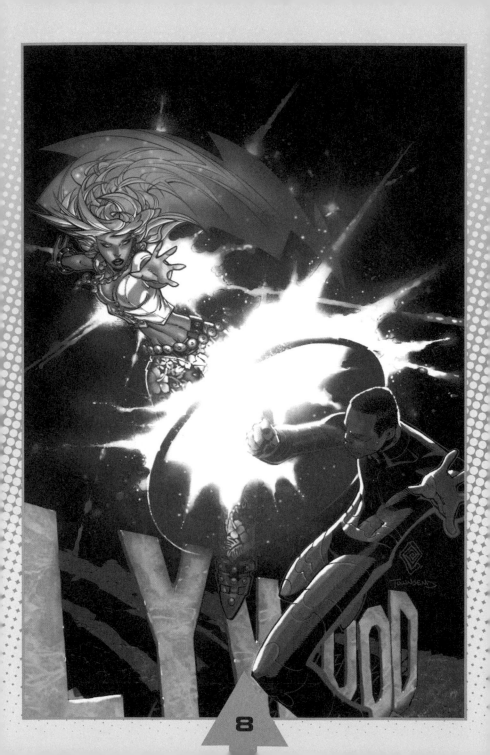

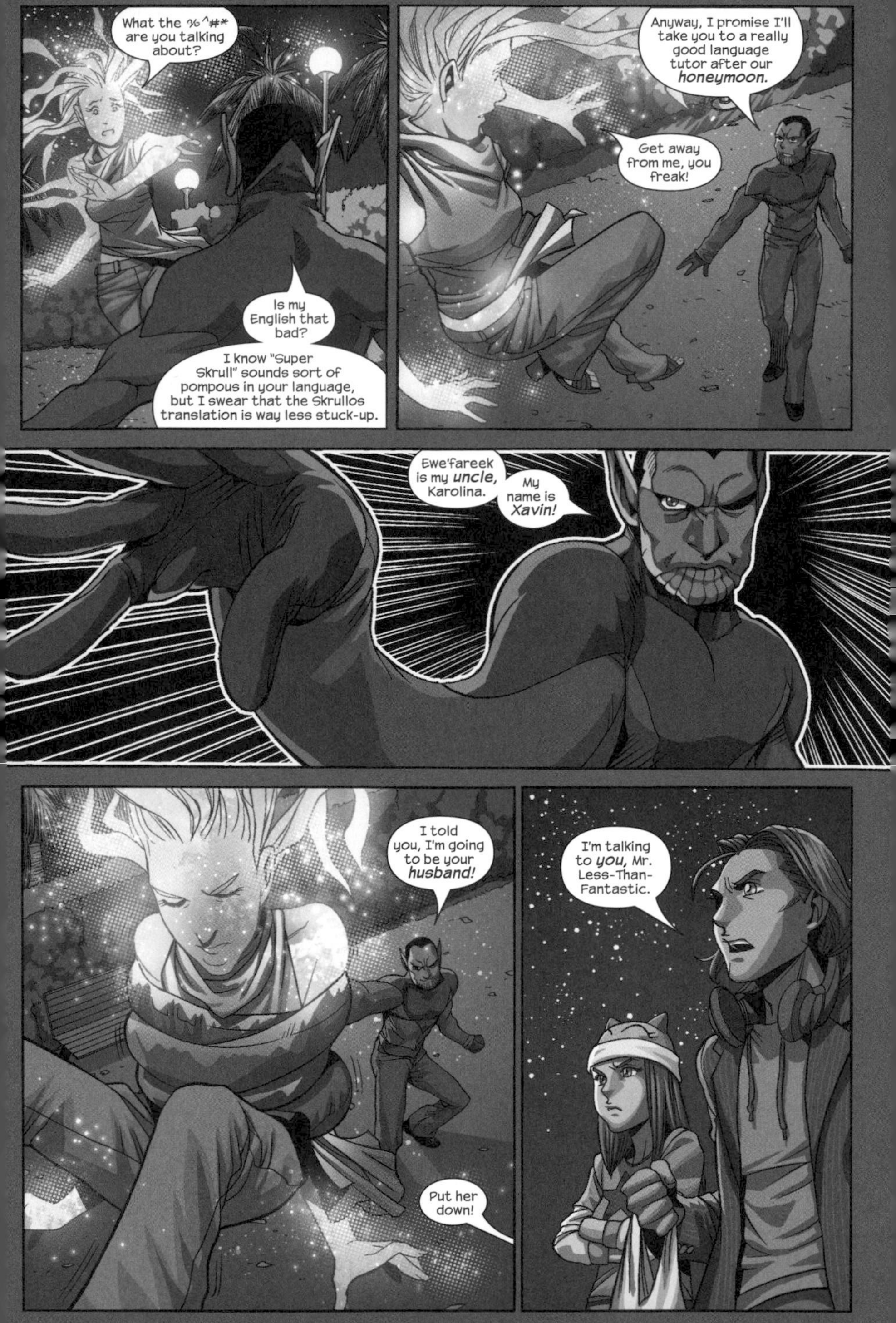
What the %^#*
are you talking
about?
Is my
English that
bad?
I know "Super
Skrull" sounds sort of
pompous in your language,
but I swear that the Skrullos
translation is way less stuck-up.
Anyway, I promise I'll
take you to a really
good language
tutor after our
honeymoon.
Get away
from me, you
freak!
Ewe'fareek
is my uncle,
Karolina.
My
name is
Xavin!
I told
you, I'm going
to be your
husband!
Put her
down!
I'm talking
to you, Mr.
Less-Than-
Fantastic.

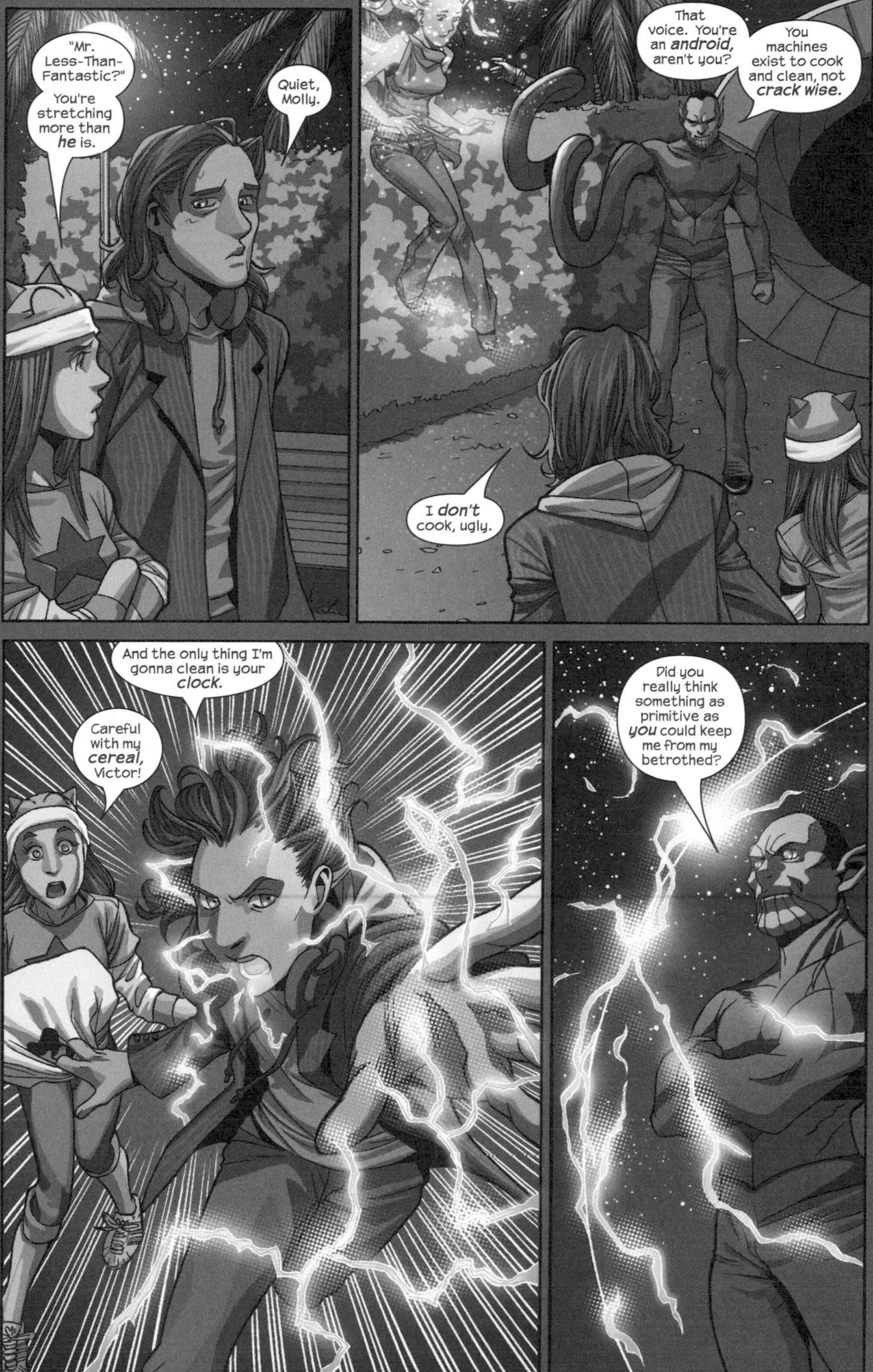
"Mr. Less-Than-Fantastic?"
You're stretching more than he is.
Quiet, Molly.
That voice. You're an android, aren't you?
You machines exist to cook and clean, not crack wise.
I don't cook, ugly.
And the only thing I'm gonna clean is your clock.
Careful with my cereal, Victor!
Did you really think something as primitive as you could keep me from my betrothed?

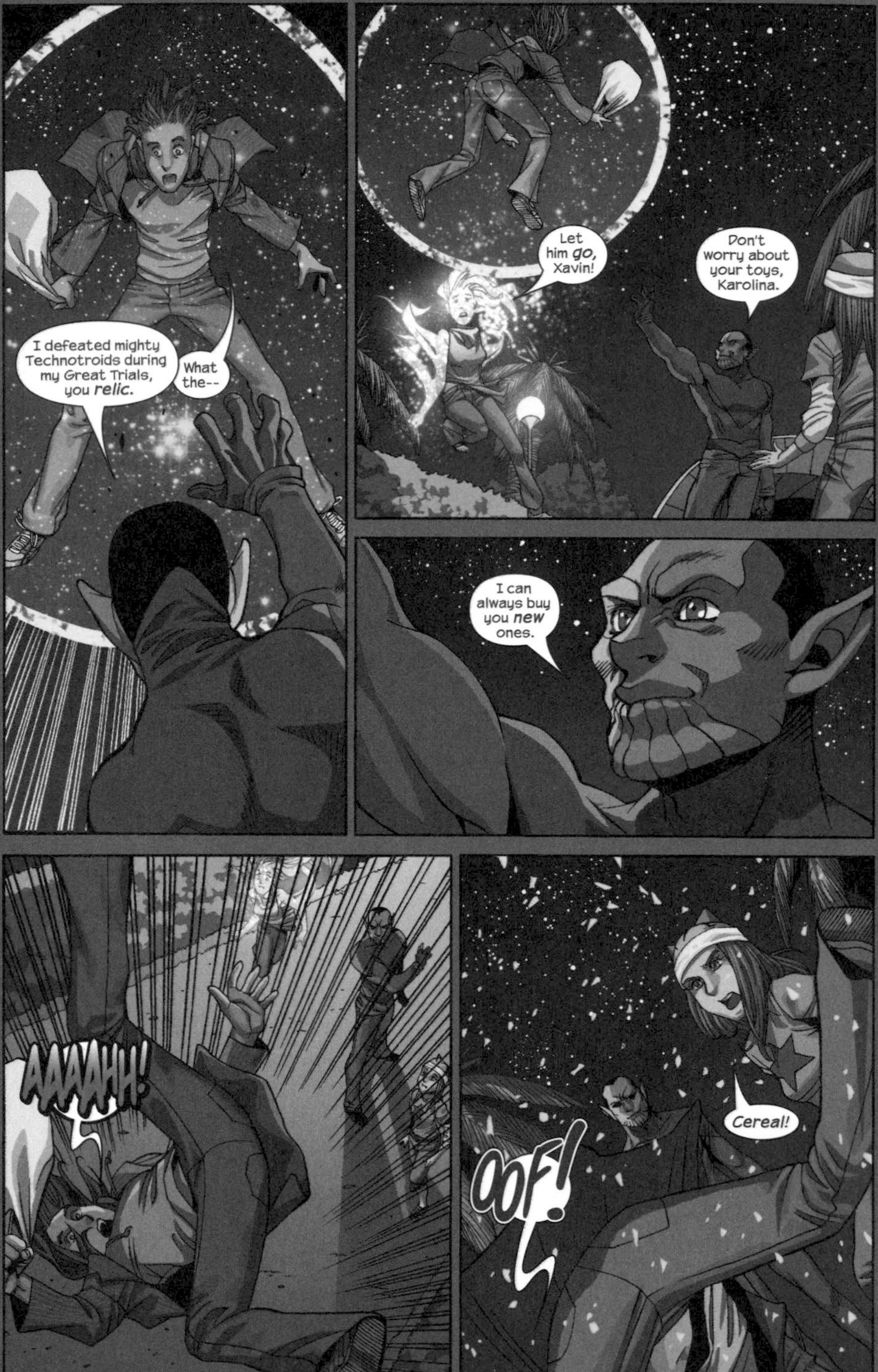
I defeated mighty Technotroids during my Great Trials, you relic.
What the--
Let him go, Xavin!
Don't worry about your toys, Karolina.
I can always buy you new ones.
AAAAHH!
Cereal!
OOF!

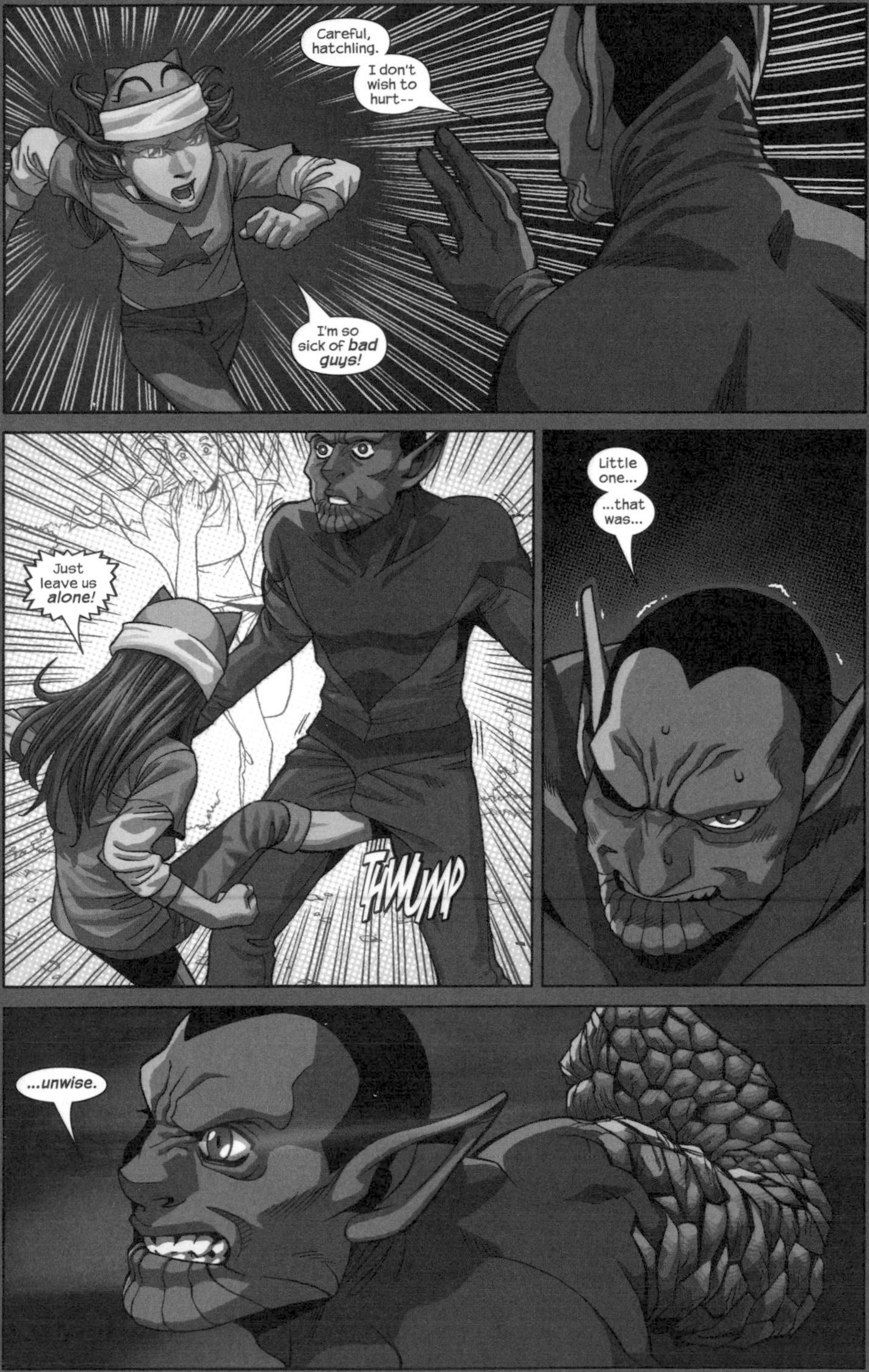

Careful, hatchling.
I don't wish to hurt--
I'm so sick of *bad guys!*
Just leave us *alone!*
THWUMP
Little one...
...that was...
...*unwise.*

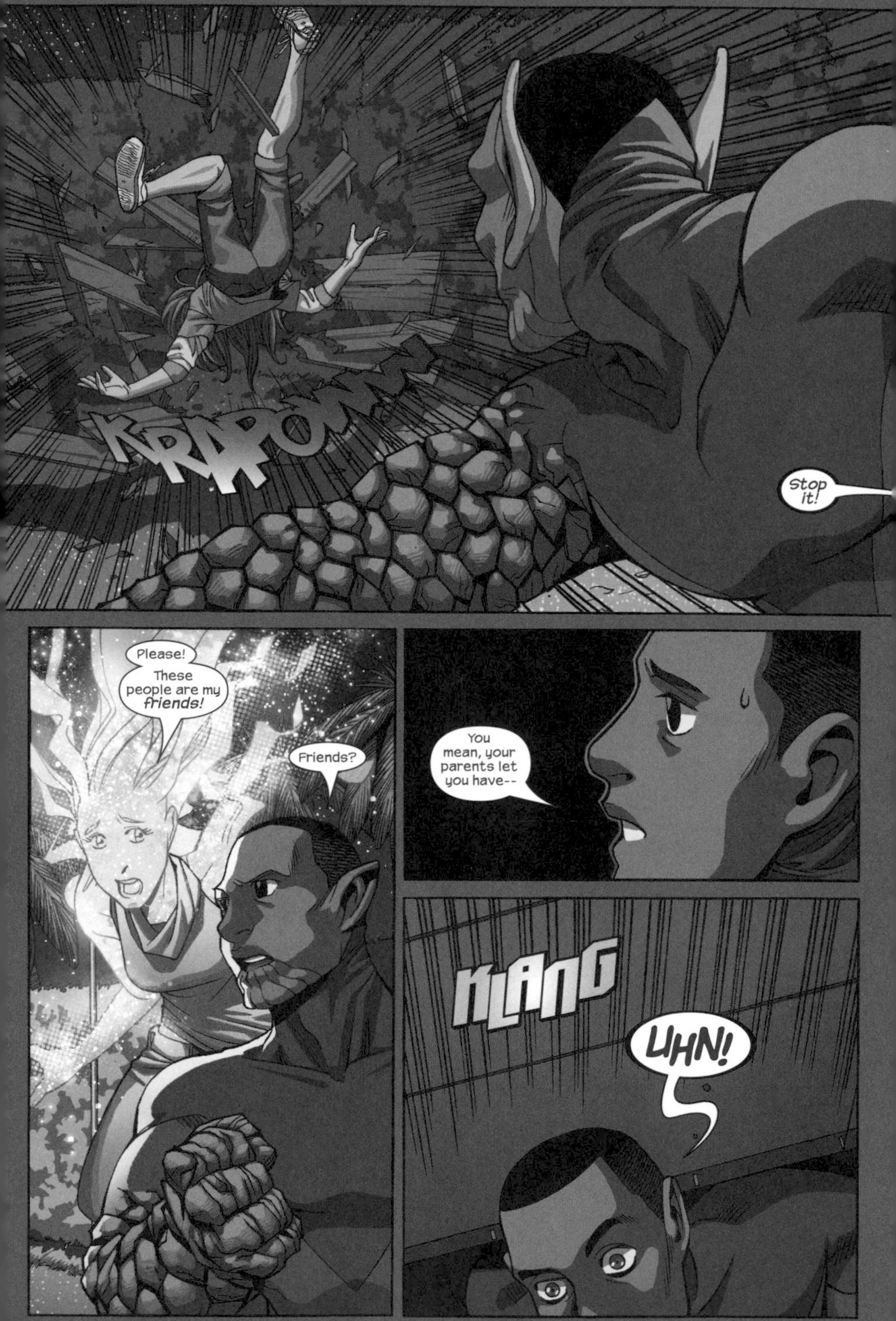
KRAPOOM
Stop it!
Please! These people are my friends!
Friends?
You mean, your parents let you have--
KLANG
UHN!

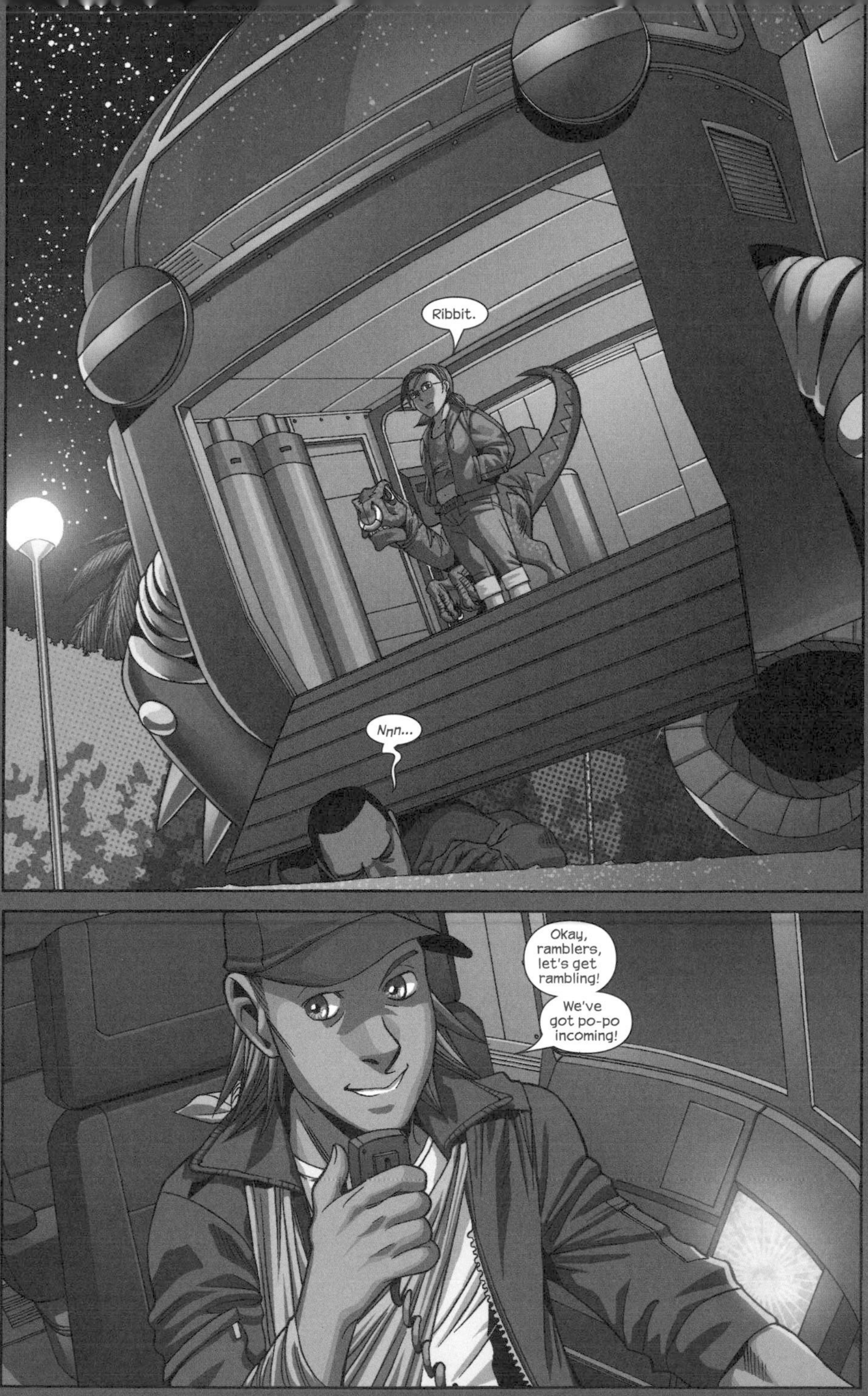
Ribbit.
Nnn...
Okay, ramblers, let's get rambling!
We've got po-po incoming!

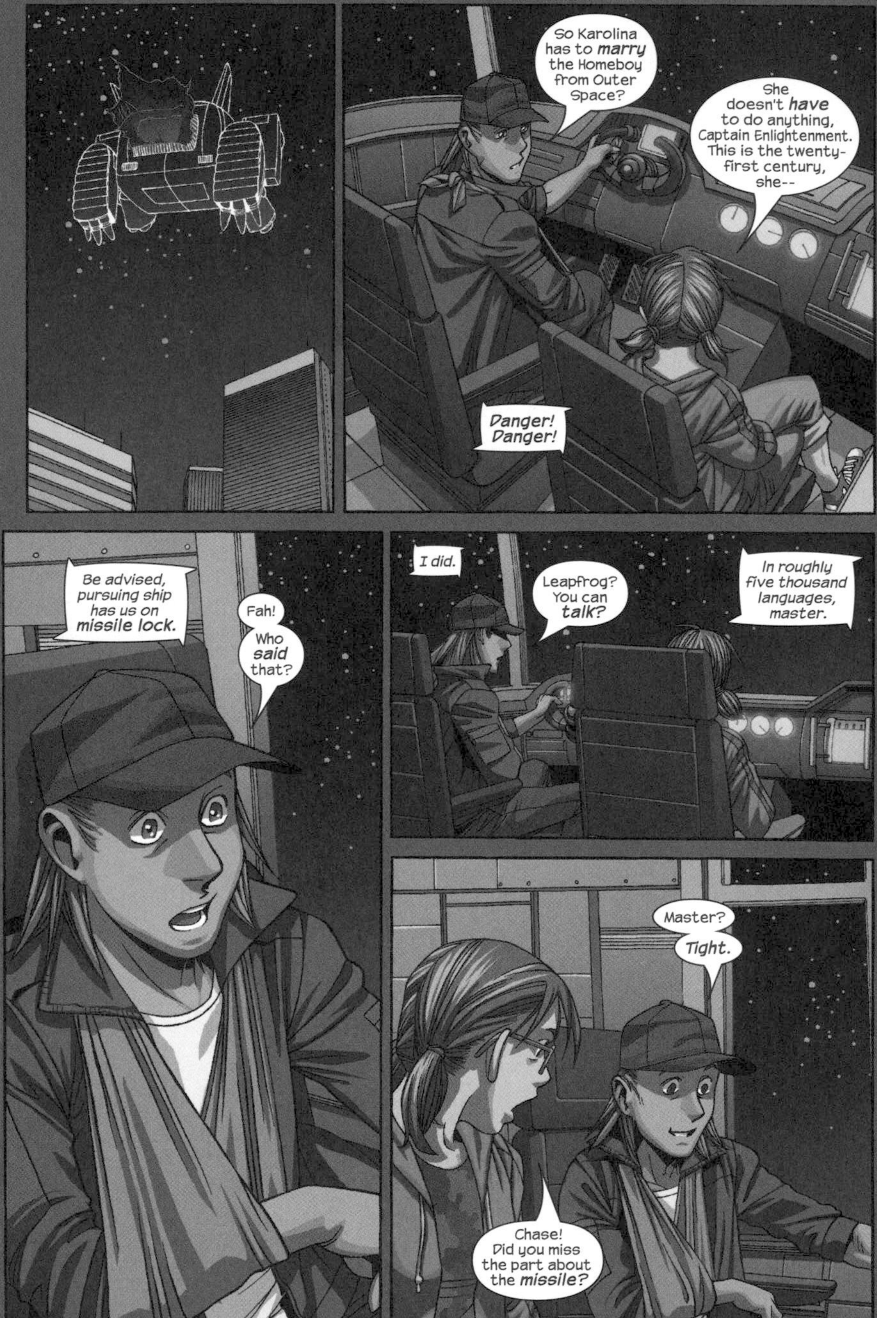
So Karolina has to *marry* the Homeboy from Outer Space?
She doesn't *have* to do anything, Captain Enlightenment. This is the twenty-first century, she--
Danger! Danger!
*Be advised, pursuing ship has us on **missile lock.***
Fah!
Who *said* that?
I did.
Leapfrog? You can *talk?*
In roughly five thousand languages, master.
Master?
Tight.
Chase! Did you miss the part about the *missile?*

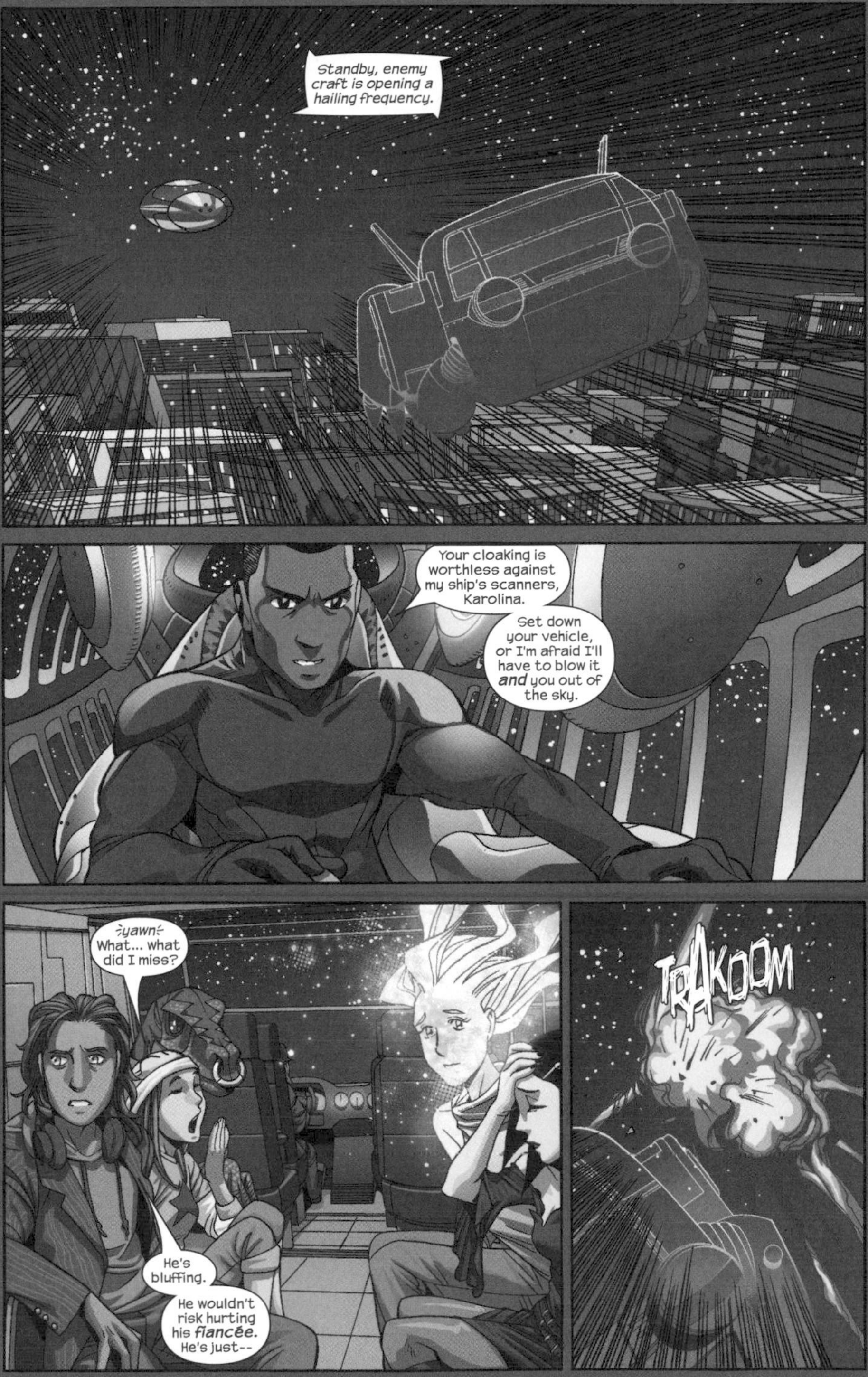
Standby, enemy craft is opening a hailing frequency.
Your cloaking is worthless against my ship's scanners, Karolina.
Set down your vehicle, or I'm afraid I'll have to blow it *and* you out of the sky.
-yawn-
What... what did I miss?
He's bluffing.
He wouldn't risk hurting his *fiancée*. He's just--
TRAKOOM

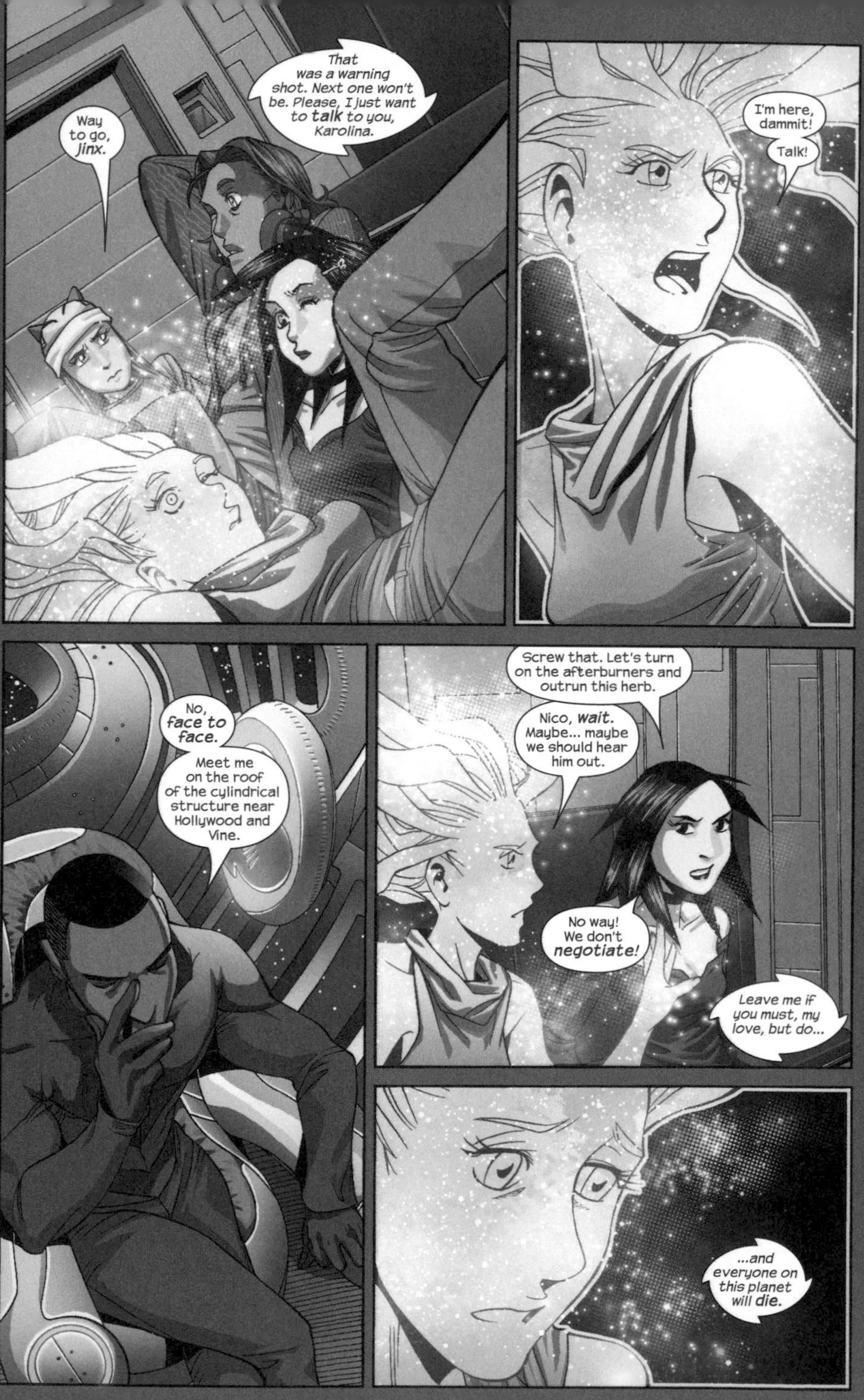

That was a warning shot. Next one won't be. Please, I just want to talk to you, Karolina.
Way to go, jinx.
I'm here, dammit!
Talk!
No, face to face.
Meet me on the roof of the cylindrical structure near Hollywood and Vine.
Screw that. Let's turn on the afterburners and outrun this herb.
Nico, wait. Maybe... maybe we should hear him out.
No way! We don't negotiate!
Leave me if you must, my love, but do...
...and everyone on this planet will die.

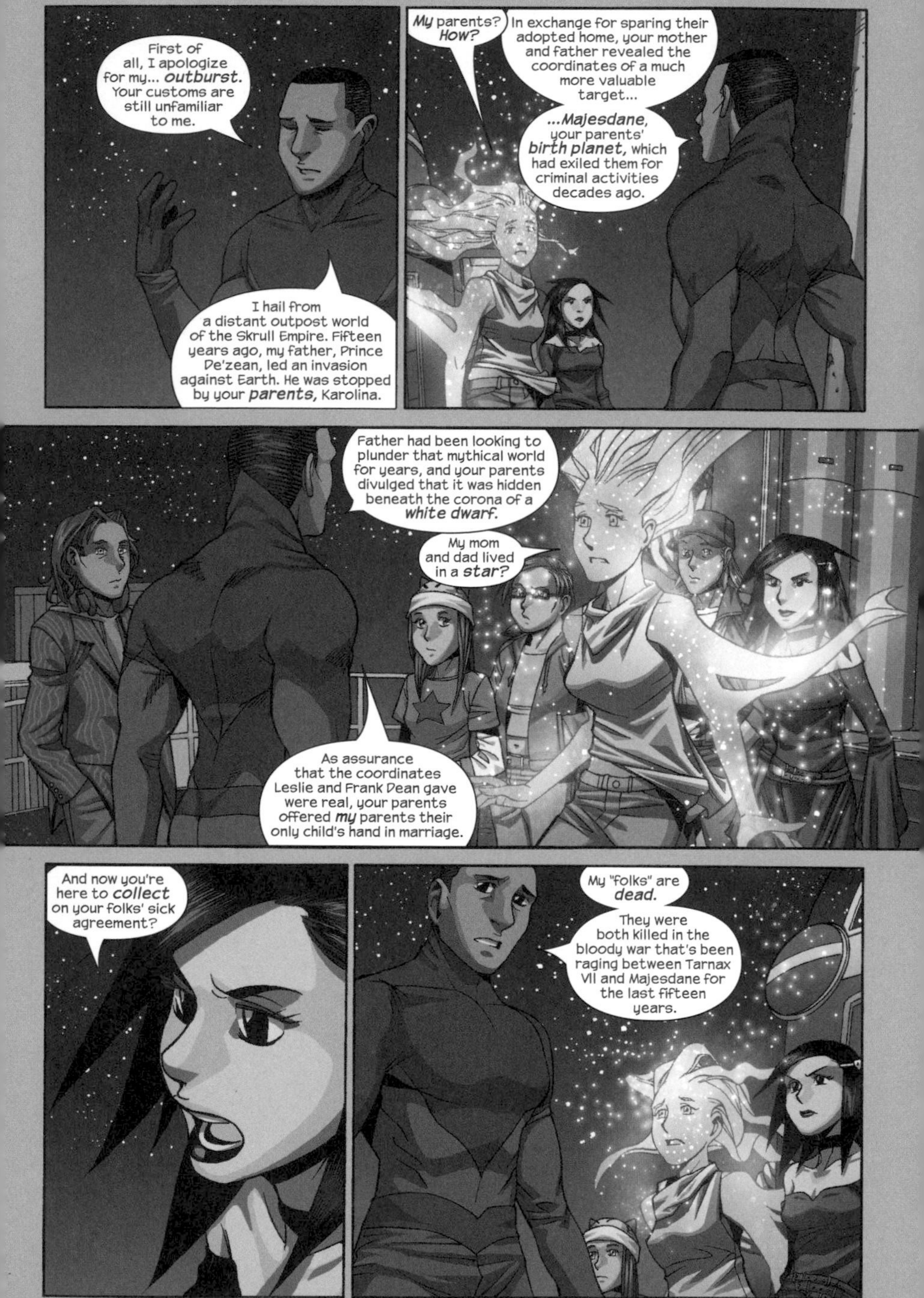
First of all, I apologize for my... outburst. Your customs are still unfamiliar to me.
I hail from a distant outpost world of the Skrull Empire. Fifteen years ago, my father, Prince De'zean, led an invasion against Earth. He was stopped by your parents, Karolina.
My parents? How?
In exchange for sparing their adopted home, your mother and father revealed the coordinates of a much more valuable target...
...Majesdane, your parents' birth planet, which had exiled them for criminal activities decades ago.
Father had been looking to plunder that mythical world for years, and your parents divulged that it was hidden beneath the corona of a white dwarf.
My mom and dad lived in a star?
As assurance that the coordinates Leslie and Frank Dean gave were real, your parents offered my parents their only child's hand in marriage.
And now you're here to collect on your folks' sick agreement?
My "folks" are dead.
They were both killed in the bloody war that's been raging between Tarnax VII and Majesdane for the last fifteen years.

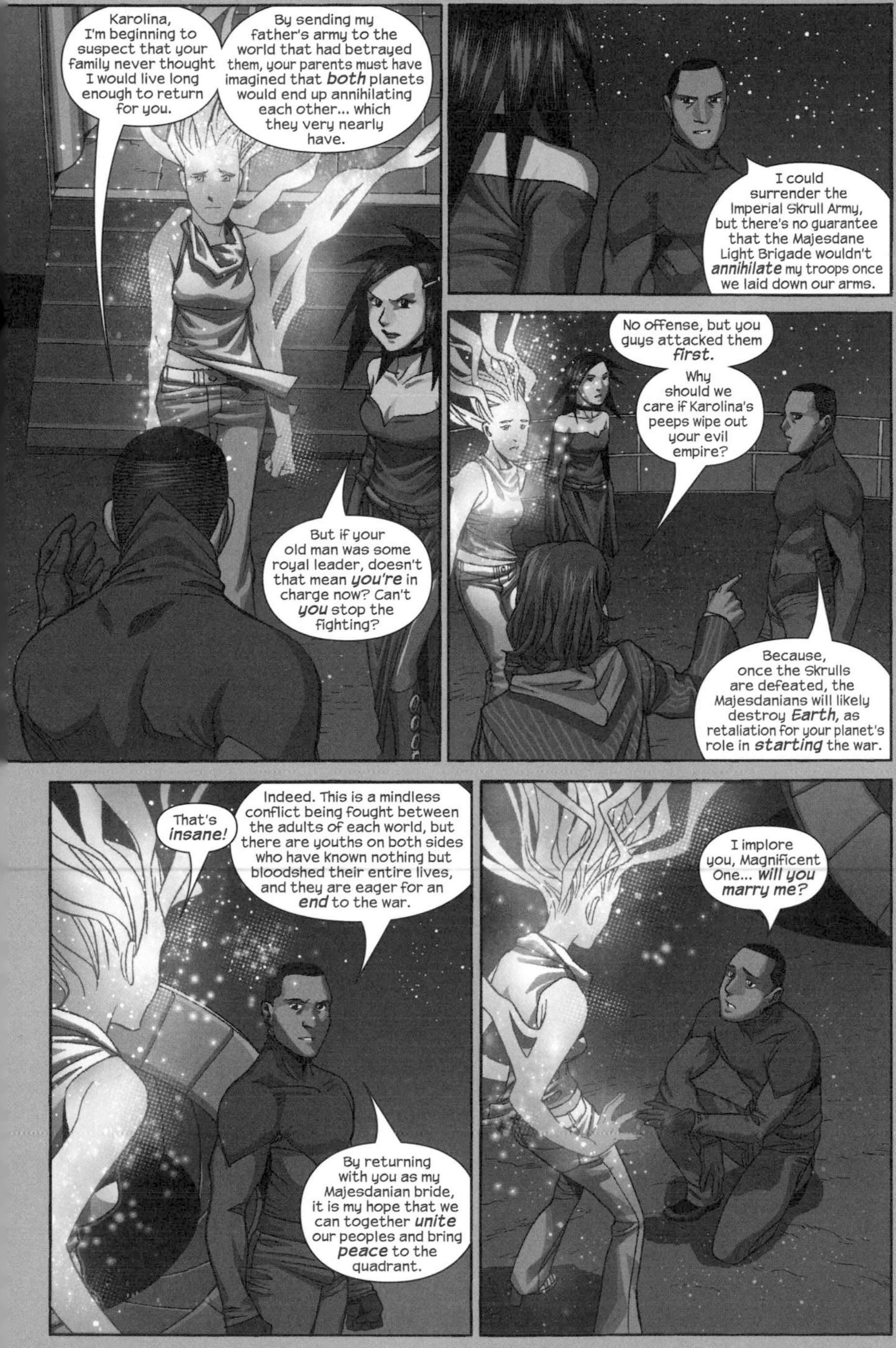
Karolina, I'm beginning to suspect that your family never thought I would live long enough to return for you.
By sending my father's army to the world that had betrayed them, your parents must have imagined that both planets would end up annihilating each other... which they very nearly have.
But if your old man was some royal leader, doesn't that mean you're in charge now? Can't you stop the fighting?
I could surrender the Imperial Skrull Army, but there's no guarantee that the Majesdane Light Brigade wouldn't annihilate my troops once we laid down our arms.
No offense, but you guys attacked them first.
Why should we care if Karolina's peeps wipe out your evil empire?
Because, once the Skrulls are defeated, the Majesdanians will likely destroy Earth, as retaliation for your planet's role in starting the war.
That's insane!
Indeed. This is a mindless conflict being fought between the adults of each world, but there are youths on both sides who have known nothing but bloodshed their entire lives, and they are eager for an end to the war.
By returning with you as my Majesdanian bride, it is my hope that we can together unite our peoples and bring peace to the quadrant.
I implore you, Magnificent One... will you marry me?

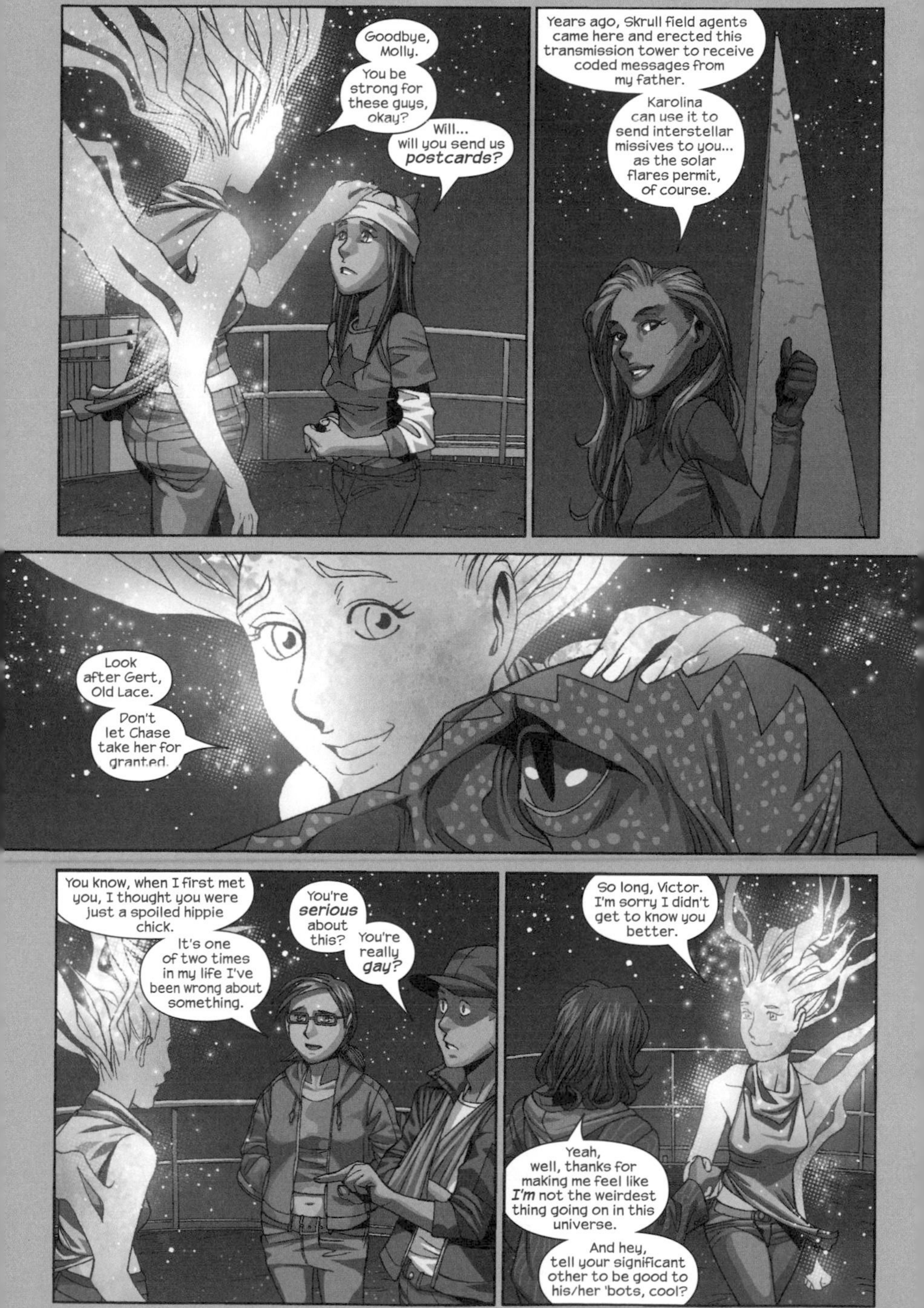

Goodbye, Molly.
You be strong for these guys, okay?
Will... will you send us postcards?
Years ago, Skrull field agents came here and erected this transmission tower to receive coded messages from my father.
Karolina can use it to send interstellar missives to you... as the solar flares permit, of course.
Look after Gert, Old Lace.
Don't let Chase take her for granted.
You know, when I first met you, I thought you were just a spoiled hippie chick.
It's one of two times in my life I've been wrong about something.
You're serious about this?
You're really gay?
So long, Victor. I'm sorry I didn't get to know you better.
Yeah, well, thanks for making me feel like I'm not the weirdest thing going on in this universe.
And hey, tell your significant other to be good to his/her 'bots, cool?

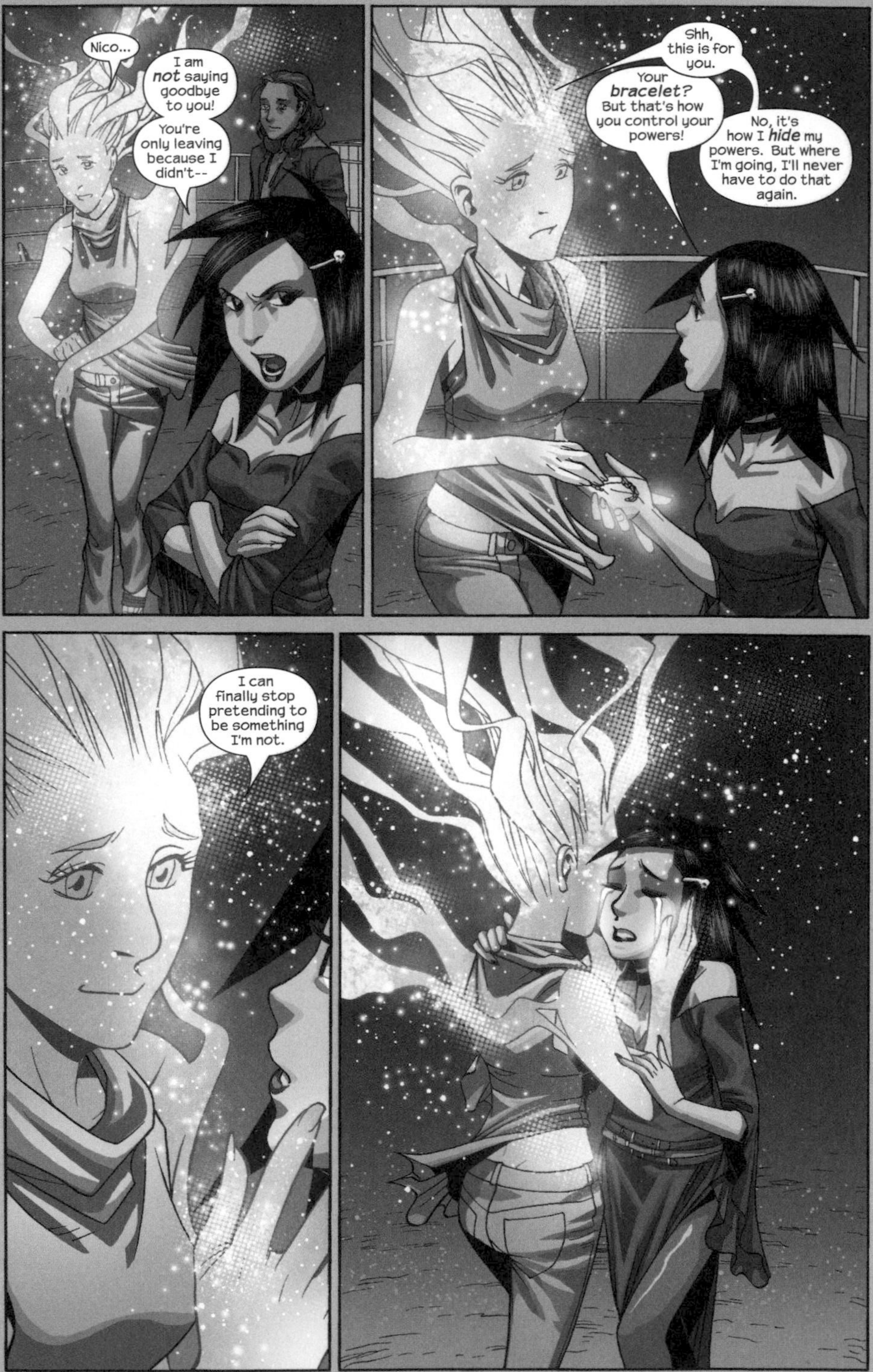
Nico...
I am *not* saying goodbye to you!
You're only leaving because I didn't--
Shh, this is for you.
Your *bracelet*? But that's how you control your powers!
No, it's how I *hide* my powers. But where I'm going, I'll never have to do that again.
I can finally stop pretending to be something I'm not.

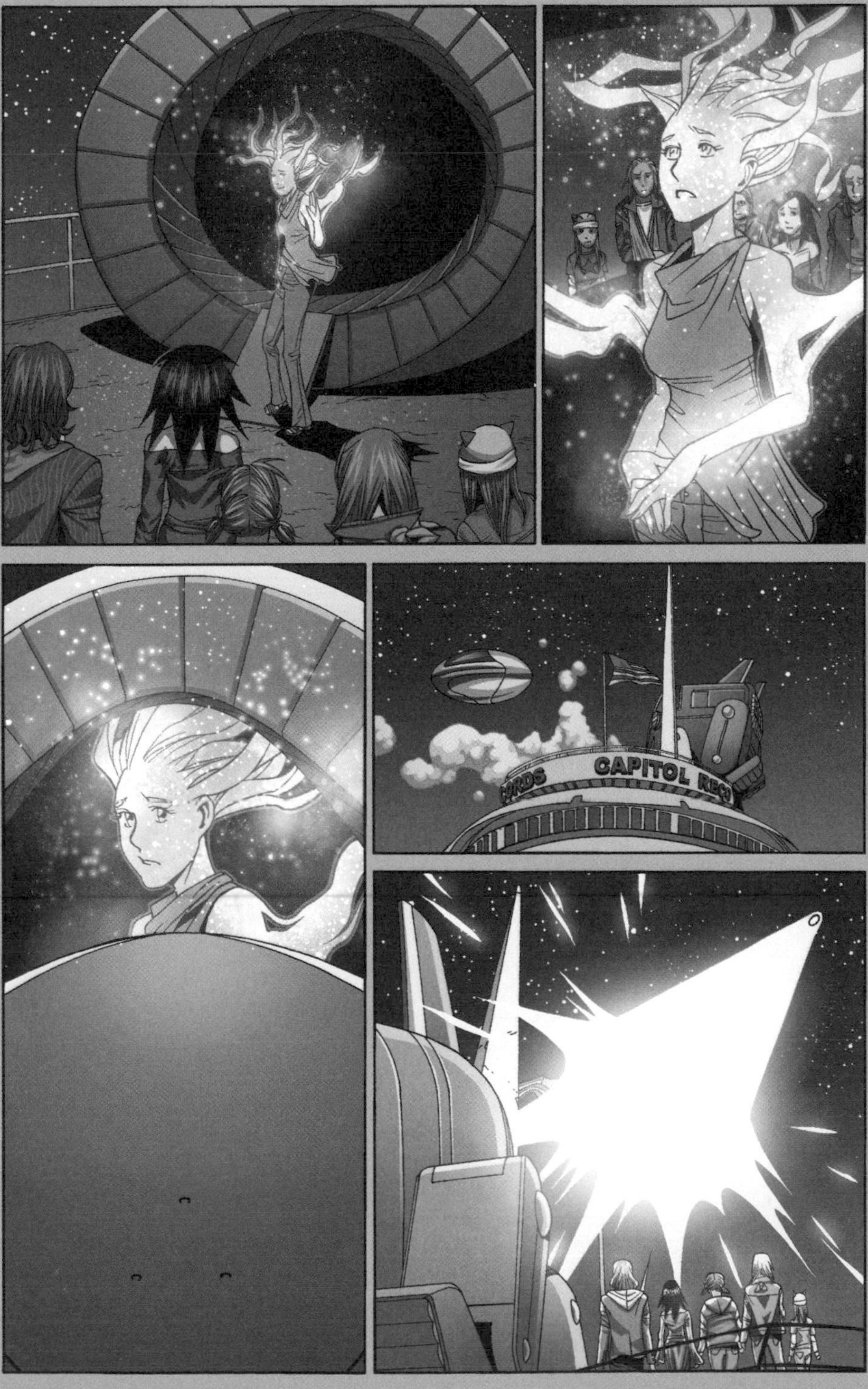
CORDS
CAPITOL REC

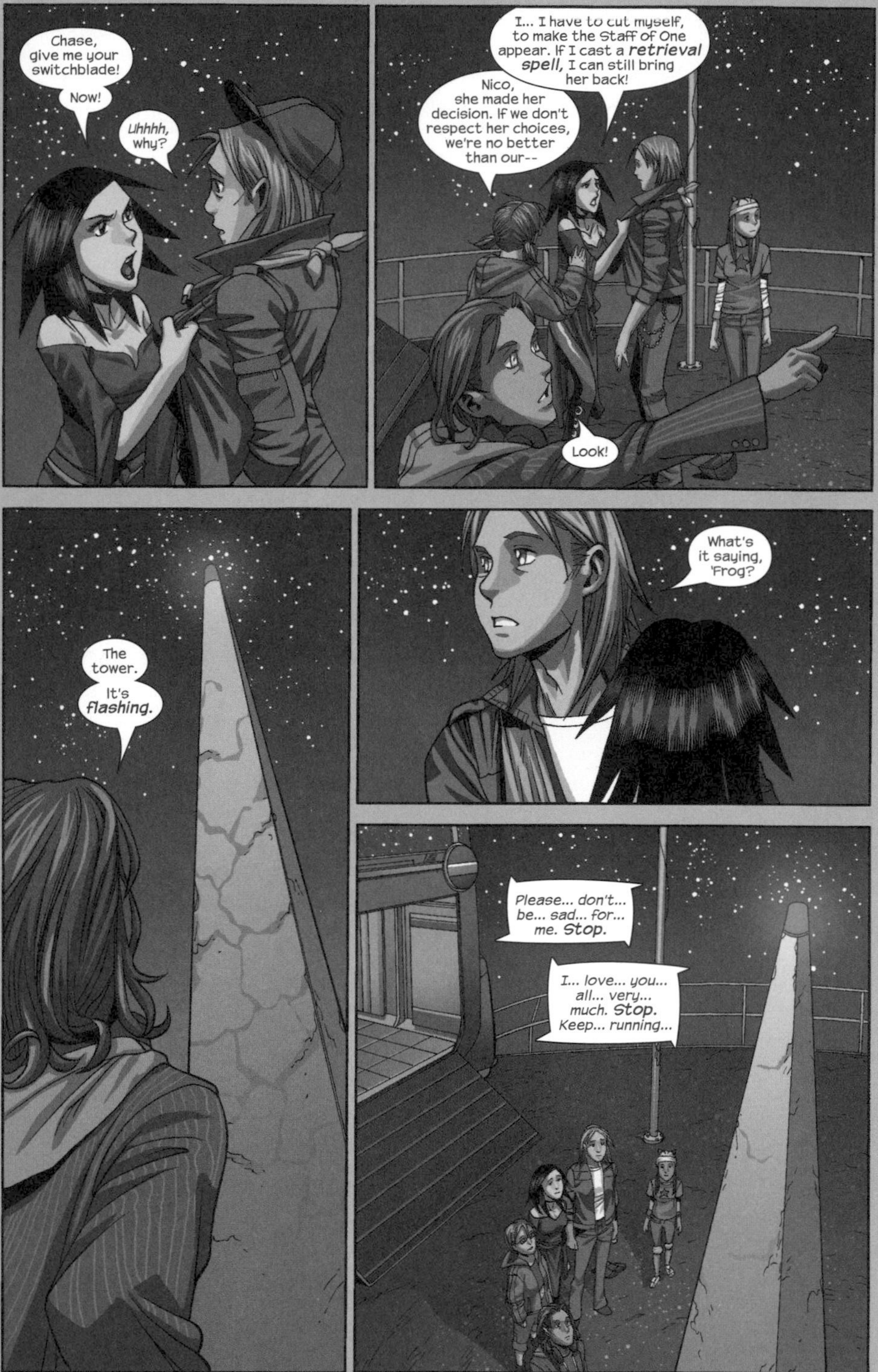
Chase, give me your switchblade!
Now!
Uhhhh, why?
I... I have to cut myself, to make the Staff of One appear. If I cast a retrieval spell, I can still bring her back!
Nico, she made her decision. If we don't respect her choices, we're no better than our--
Look!
The tower.
It's flashing.
What's it saying, 'Frog?
Please... don't... be... sad... for... me. Stop.
I... love... you... all... very... much. Stop. Keep... running...

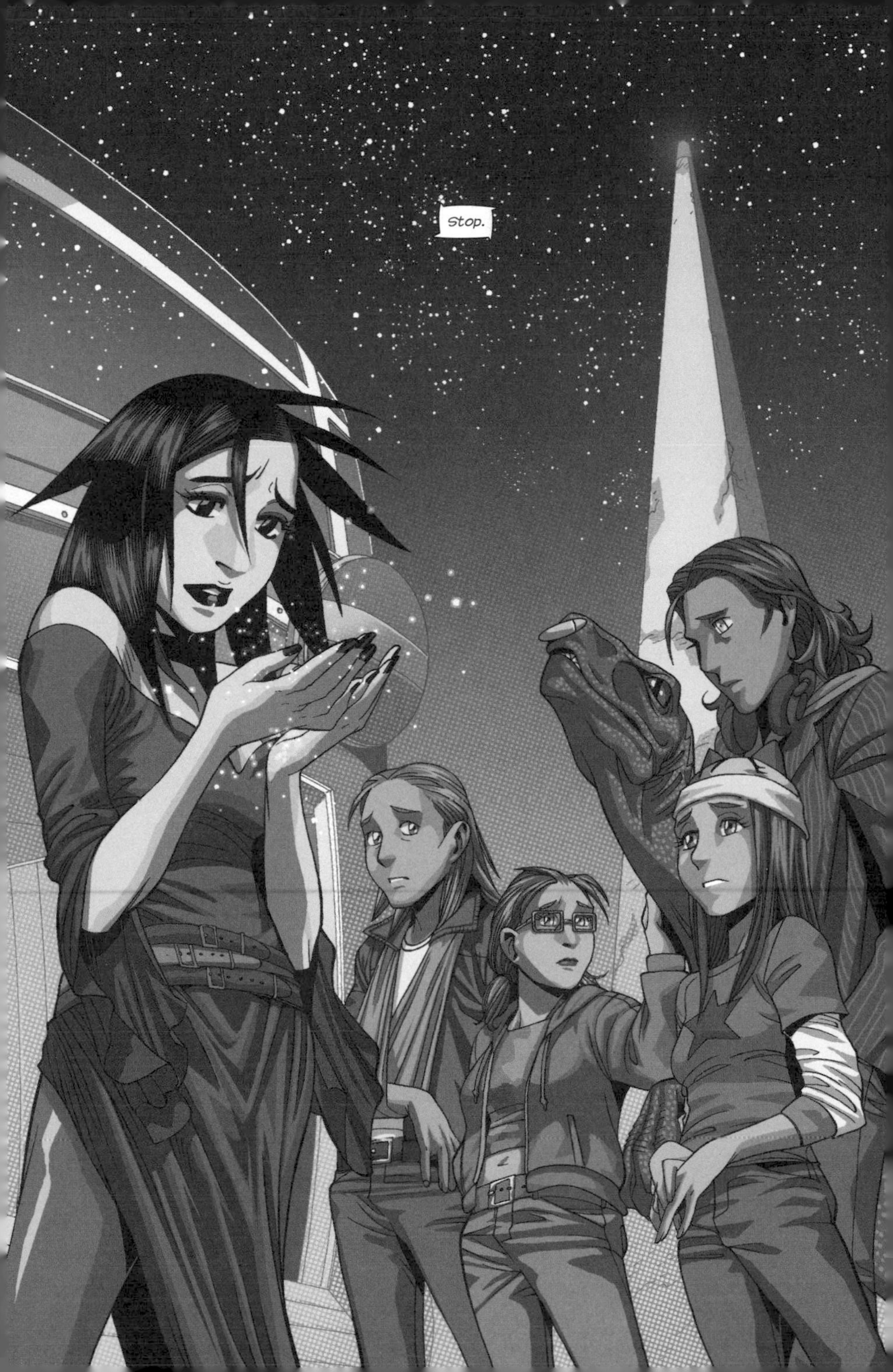
Stop.

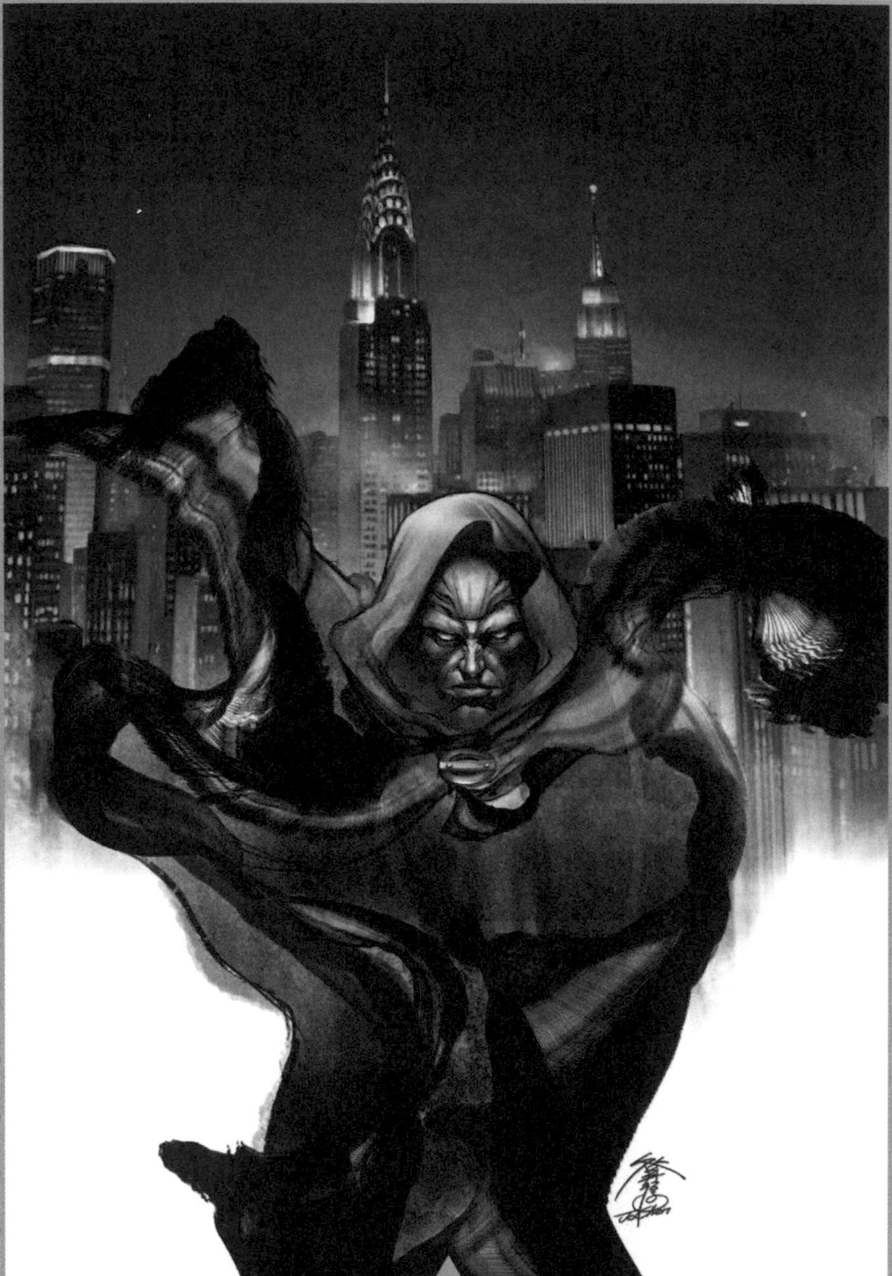

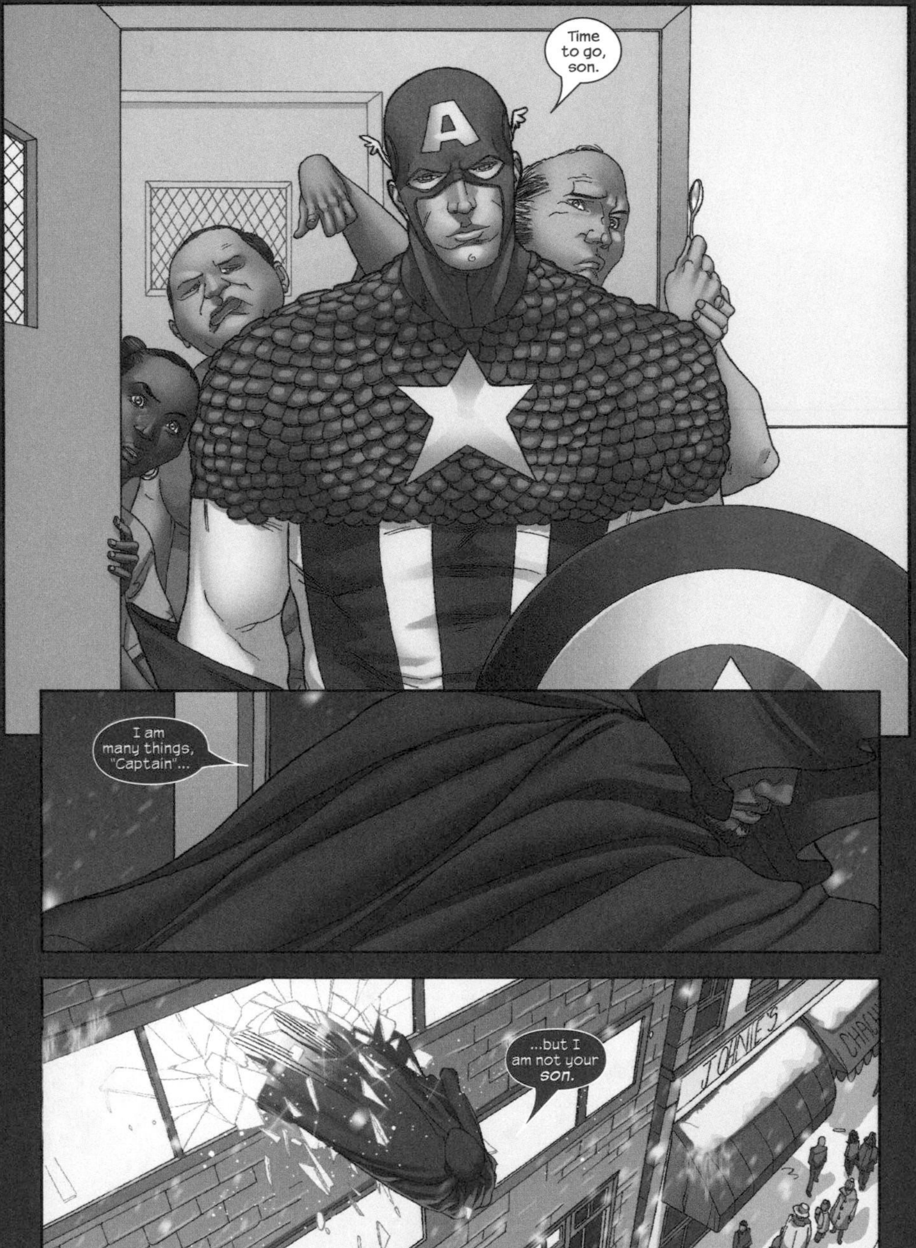
Time to go, son.
I am many things, "Captain"...
...but I am not your *son.*
JOHNIE'S
CHA

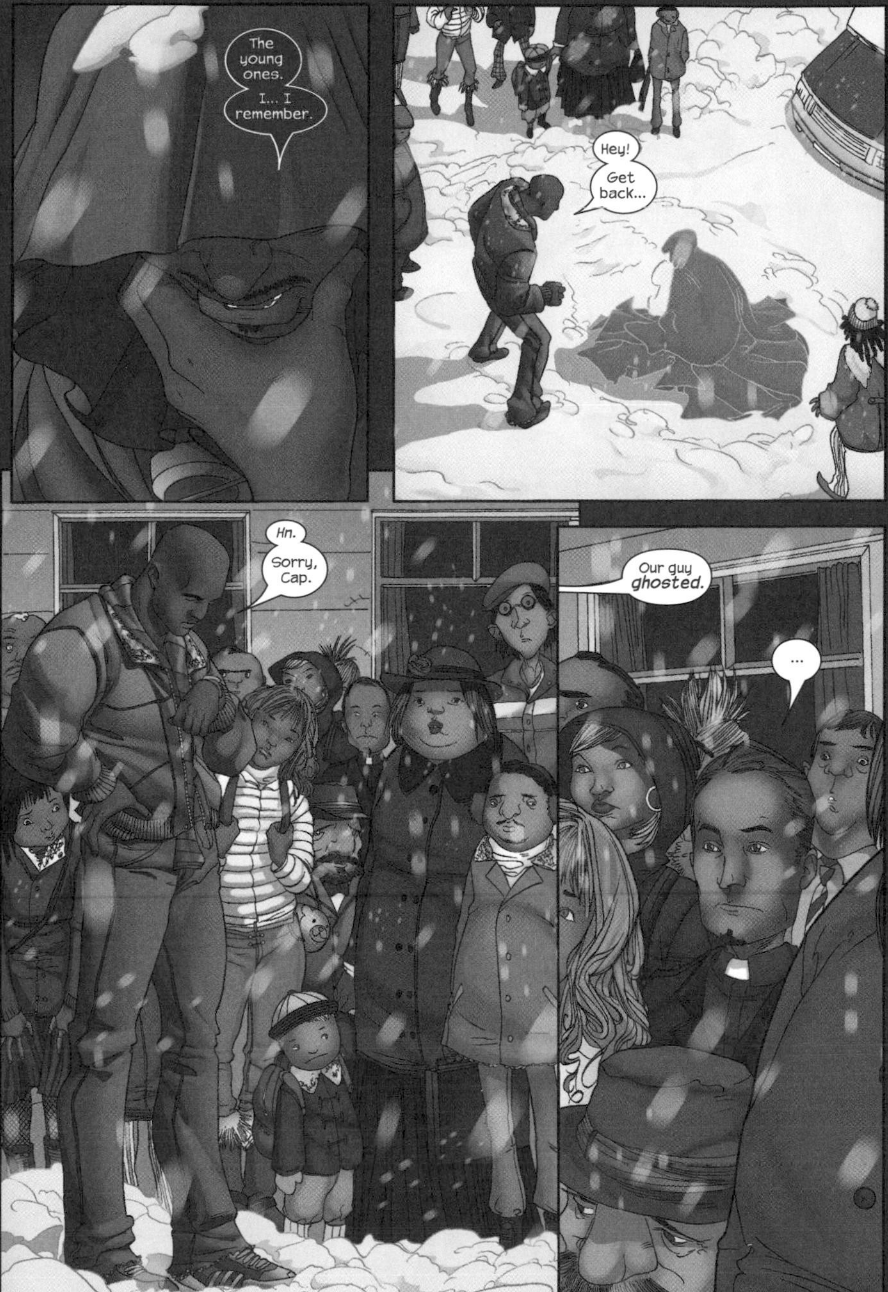
The young ones.
I... I remember.
Hey!
Get back...
Hn.
Sorry, Cap.
Our guy *ghosted*.
...

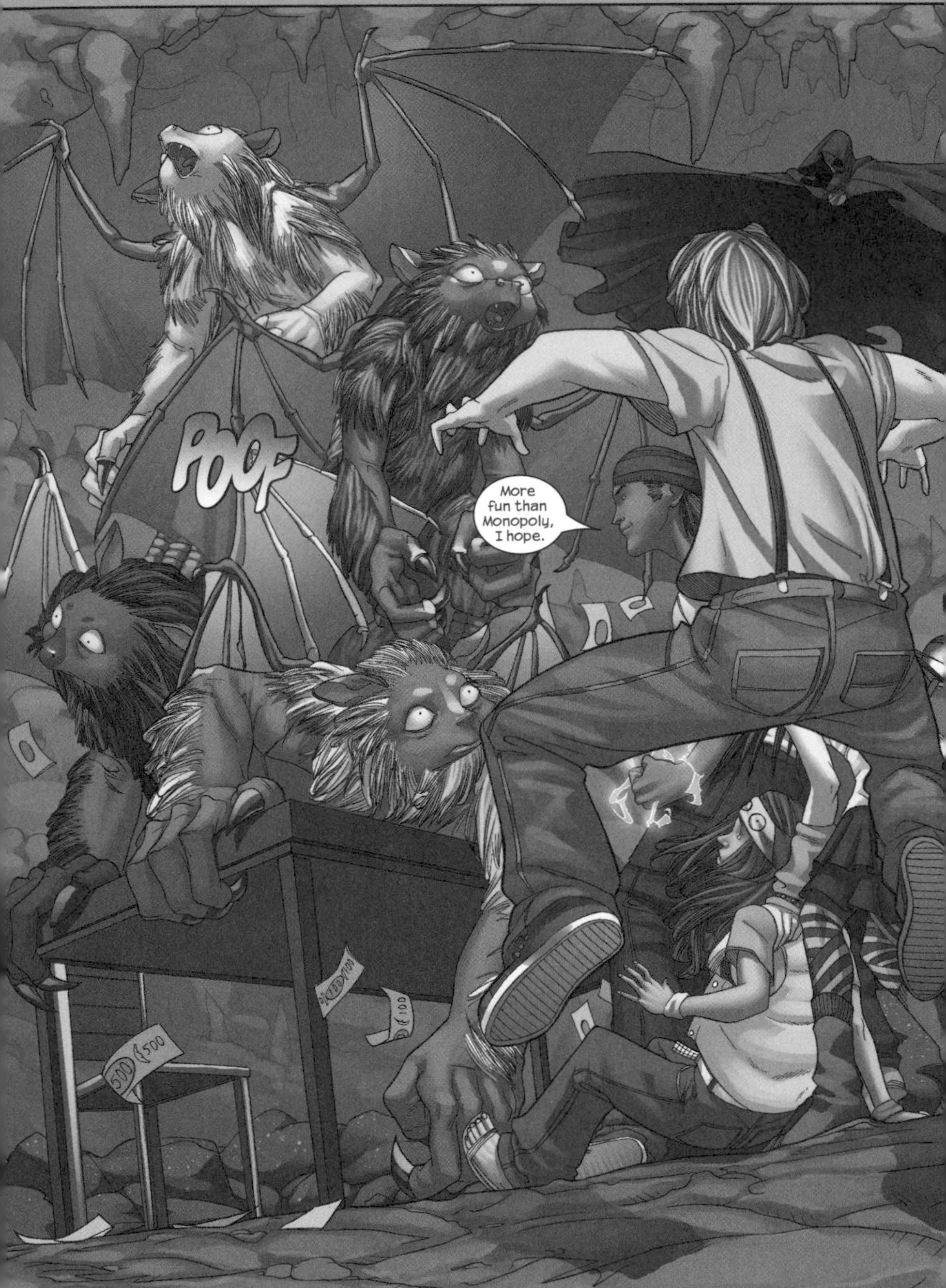
POOF
More fun than Monopoly, I hope.

10

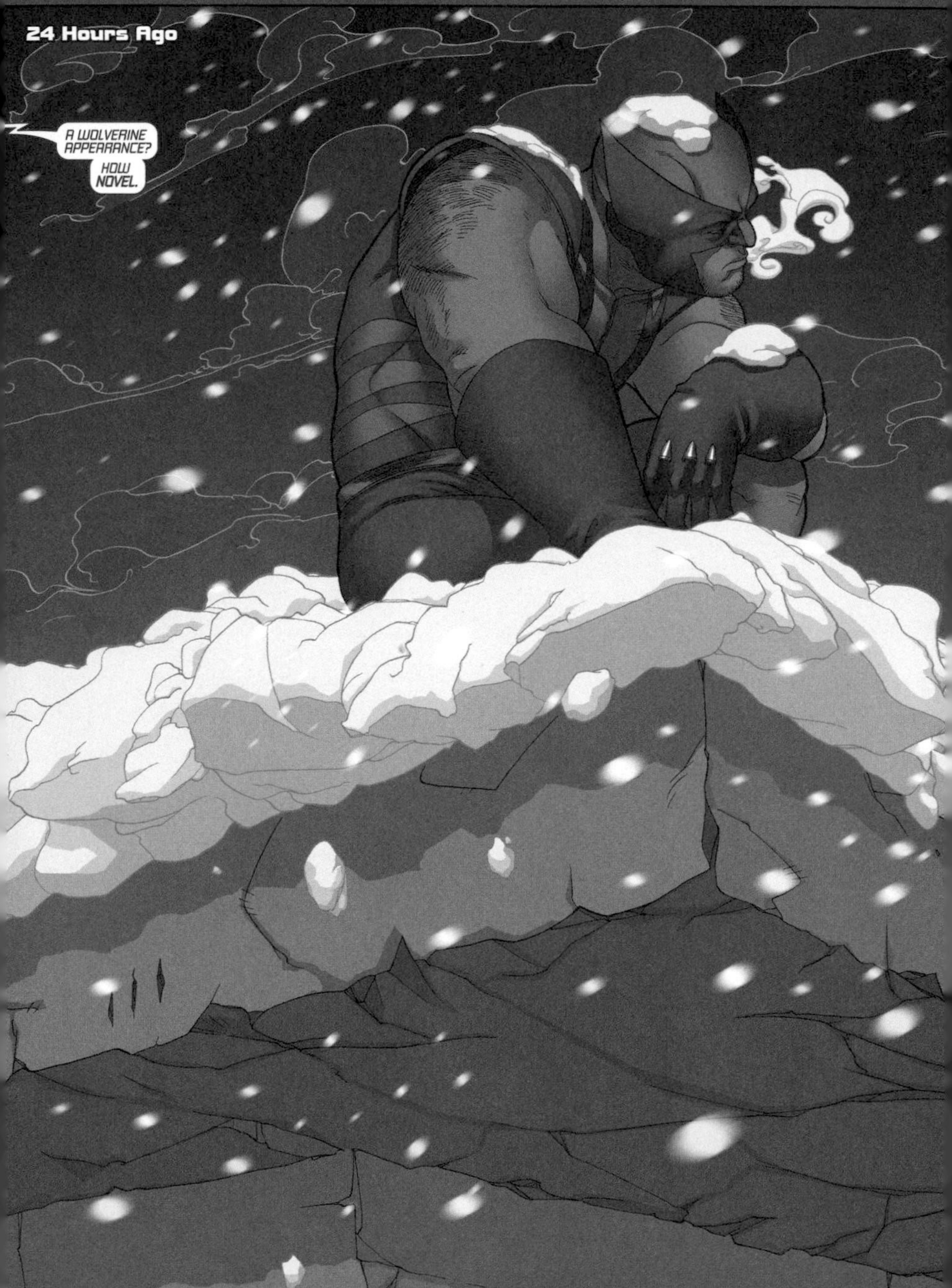
24 Hours Ago
A WOLVERINE APPEARANCE? HOW NOVEL.

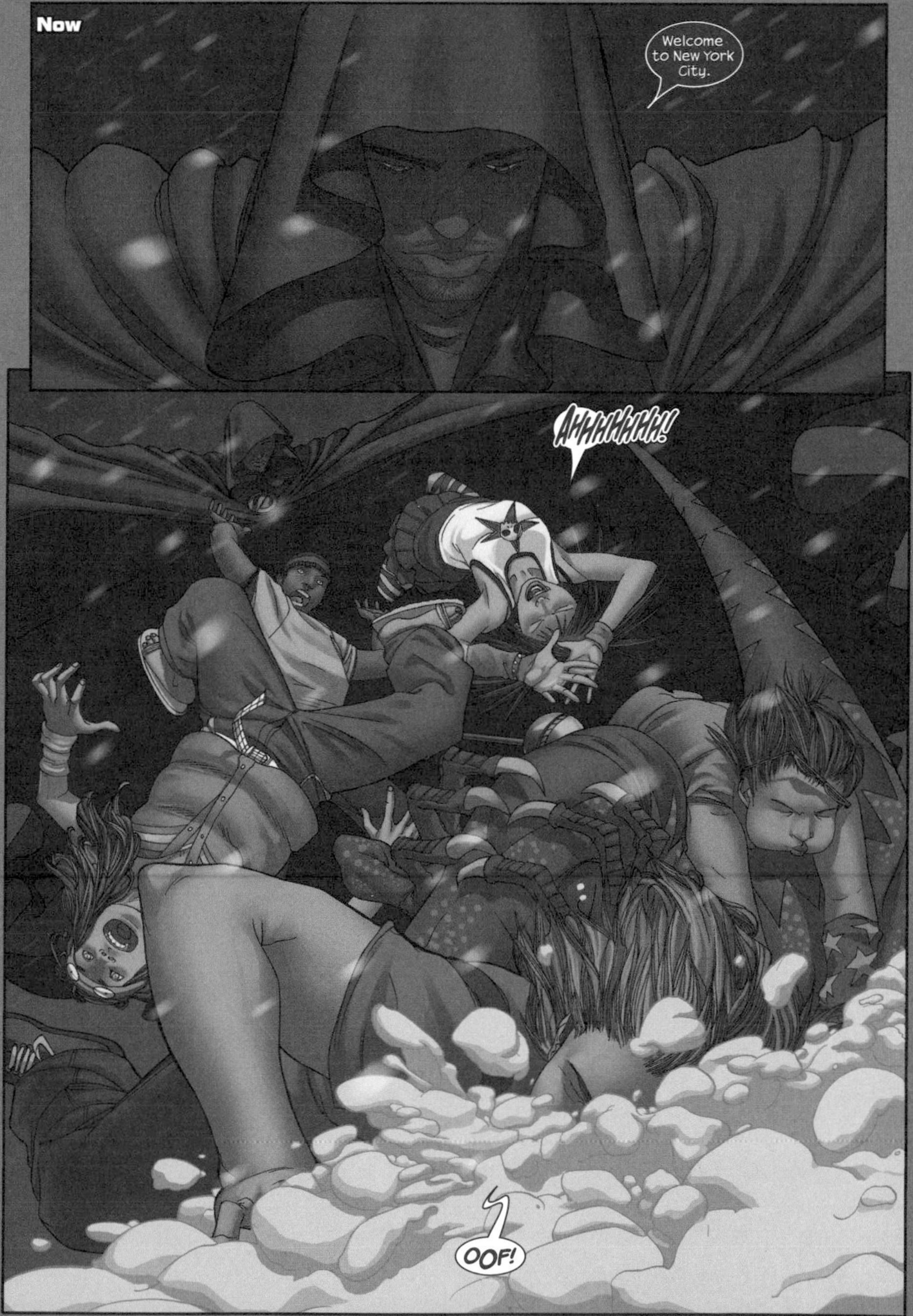
Now
Welcome to New York City.
AHHHHHHH!
OOF!

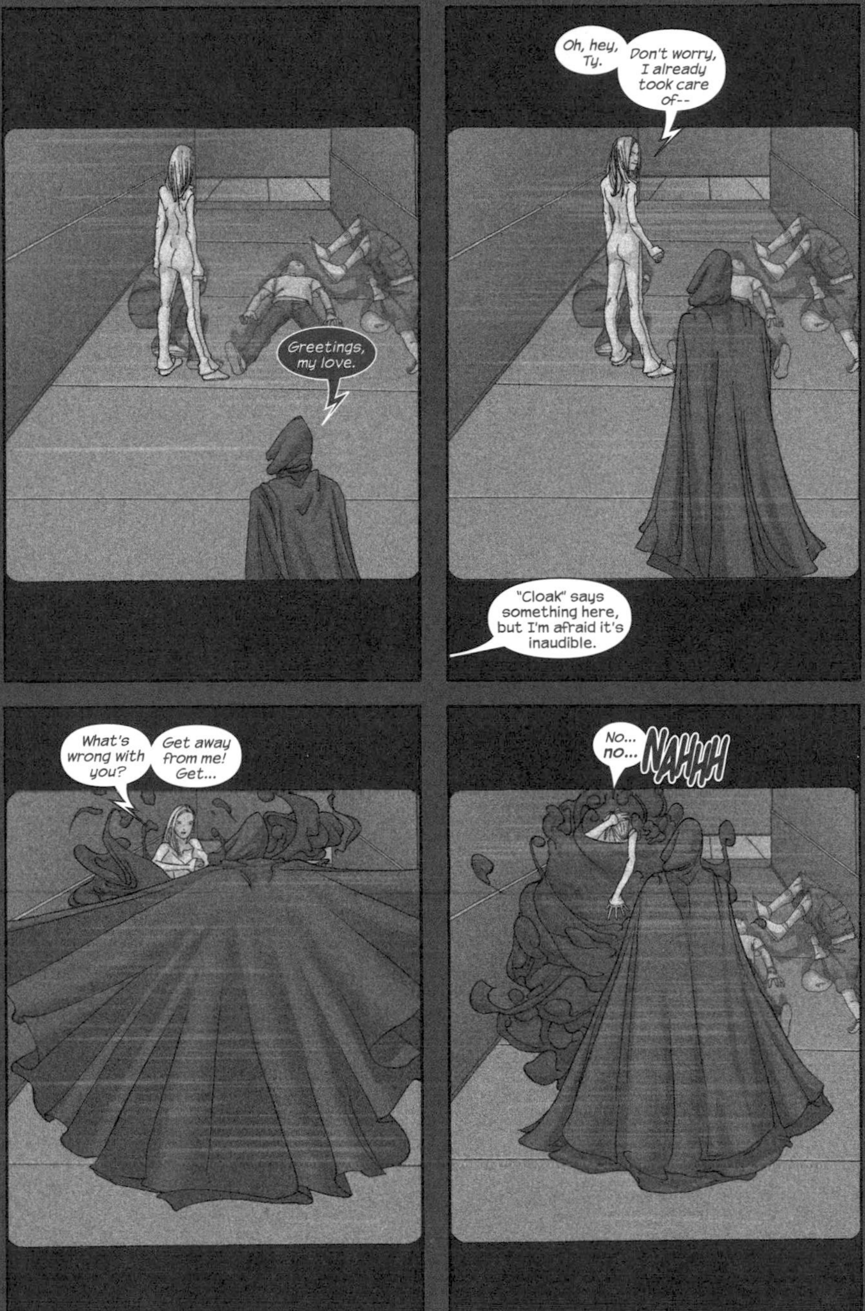
Greetings, my love.
Oh, hey, Ty.
Don't worry, I already took care of--
"Cloak" says something here, but I'm afraid it's inaudible.
What's wrong with you?
Get away from me! Get...
No... no...
NAHHH

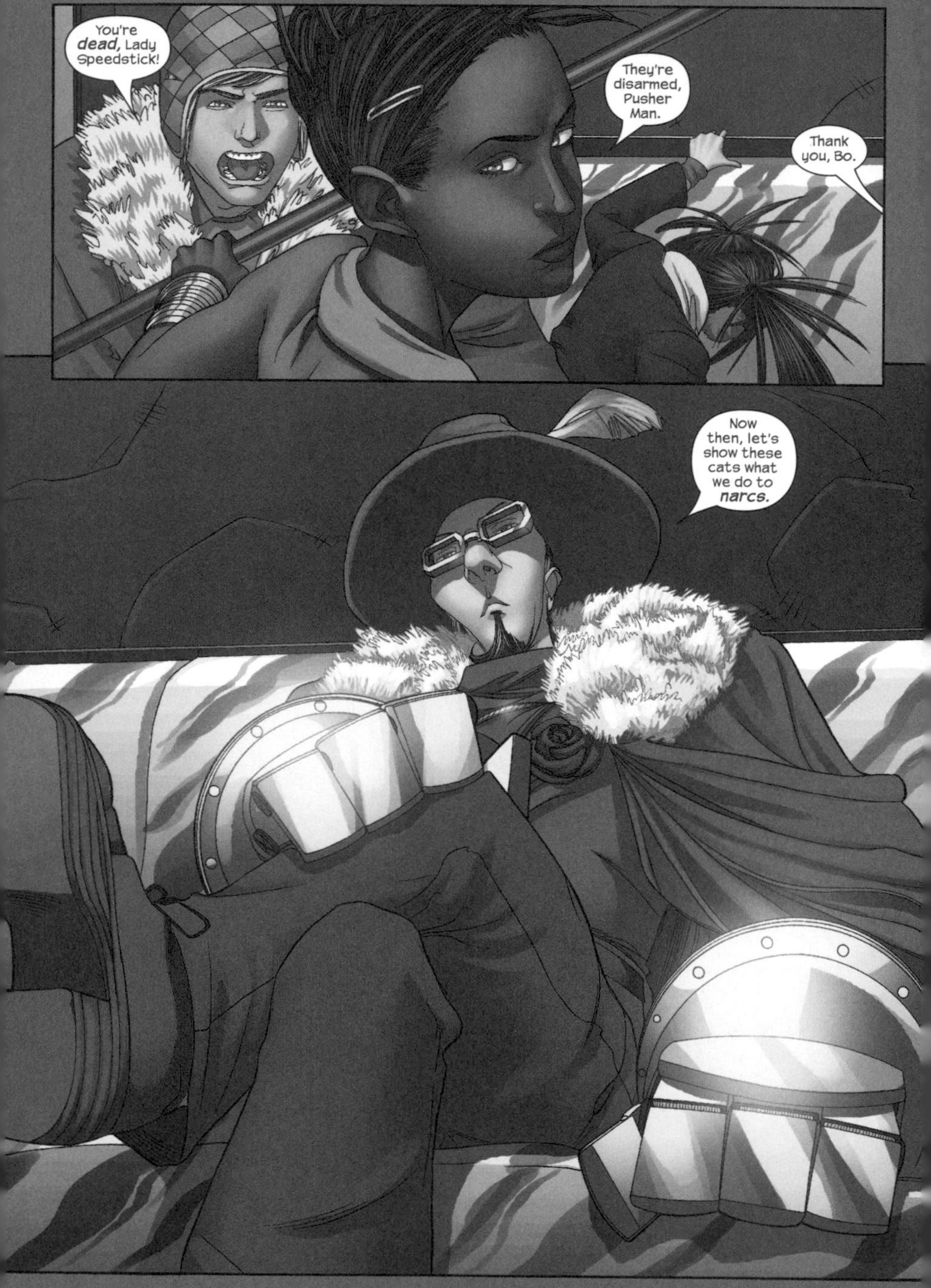
You're *dead,* Lady Speedstick!
They're disarmed, Pusher Man.
Thank you, Bo.
Now then, let's show these cats what we do to *narcs.*

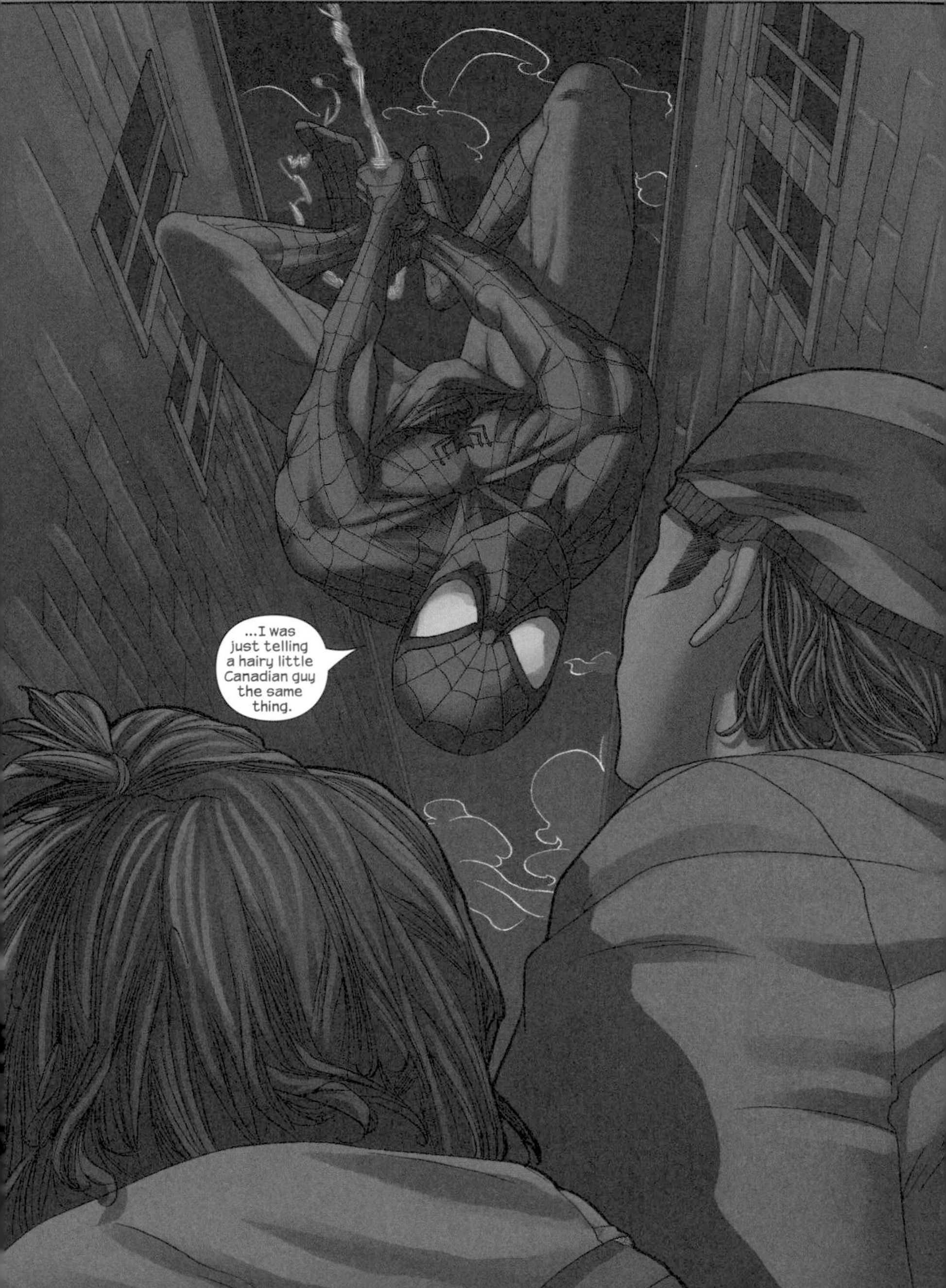
...I was just telling a hairy little Canadian guy the same thing.

11

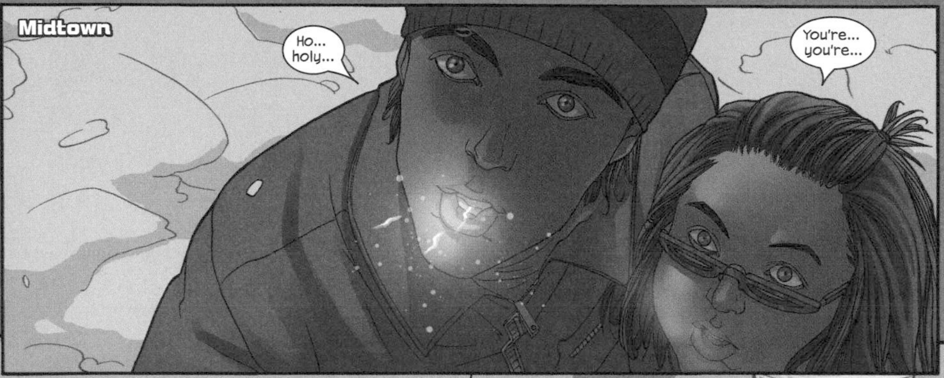
Midtown
Ho... holy...
You're... you're...

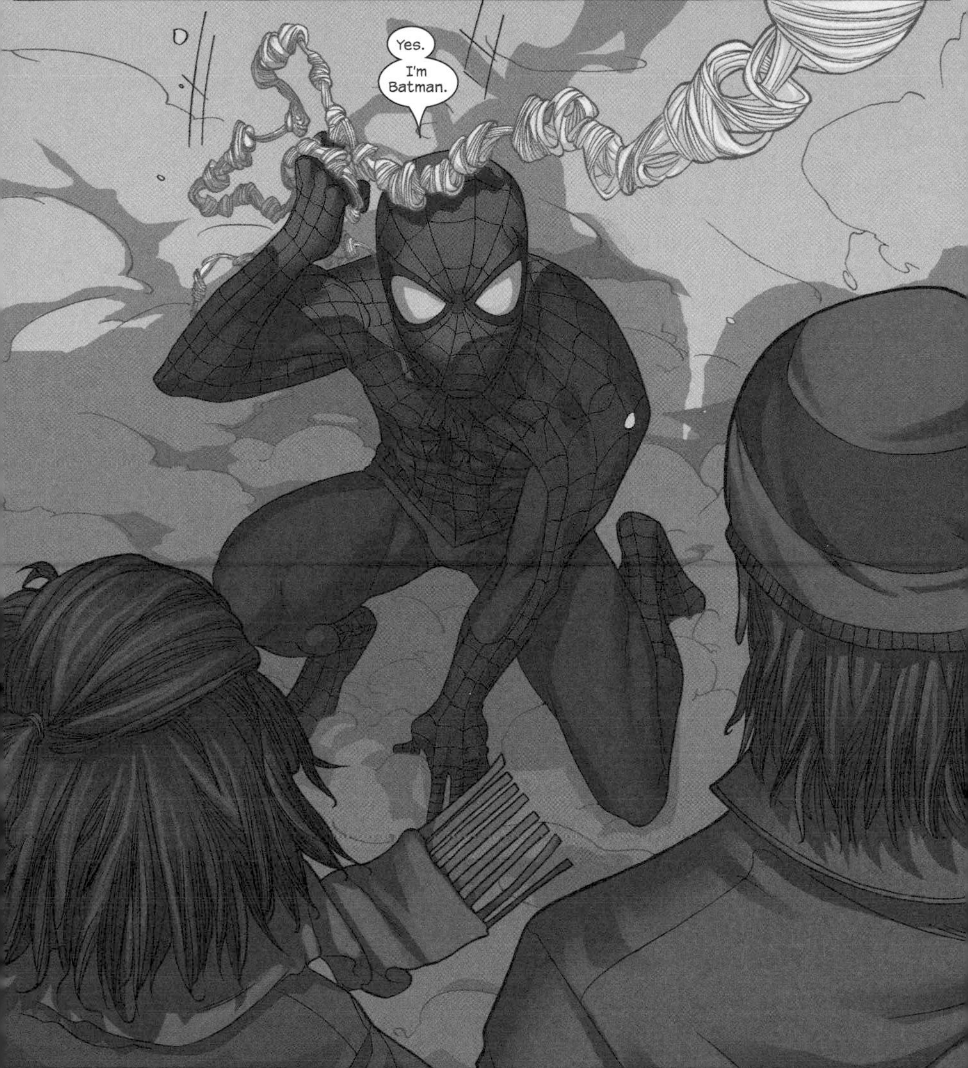
Yes.
I'm Batman.

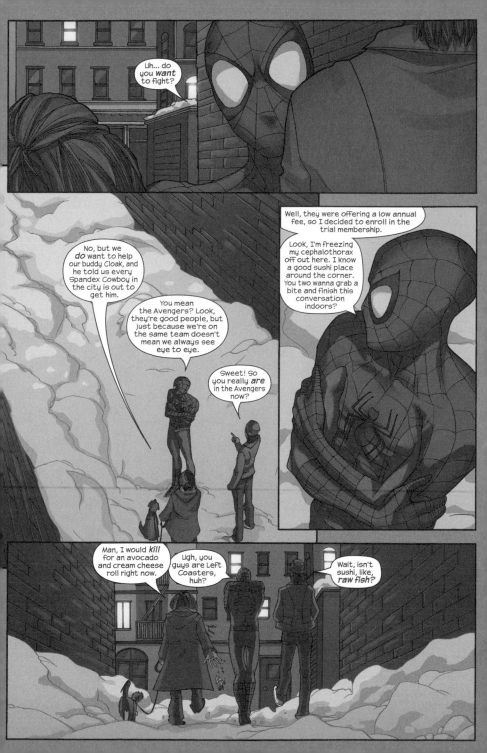

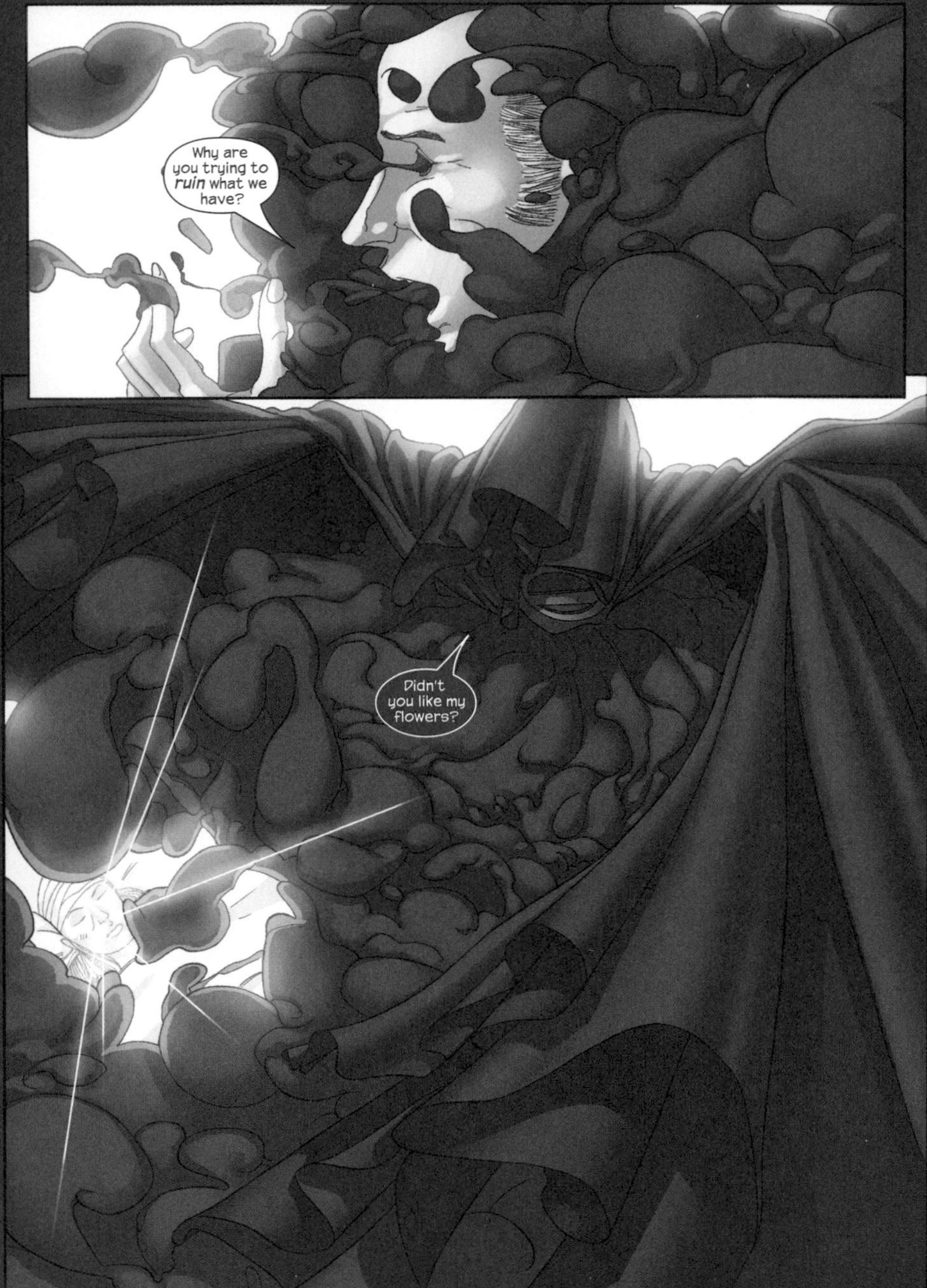
Why are you trying to *ruin* what we have?
Didn't you like my flowers?

12

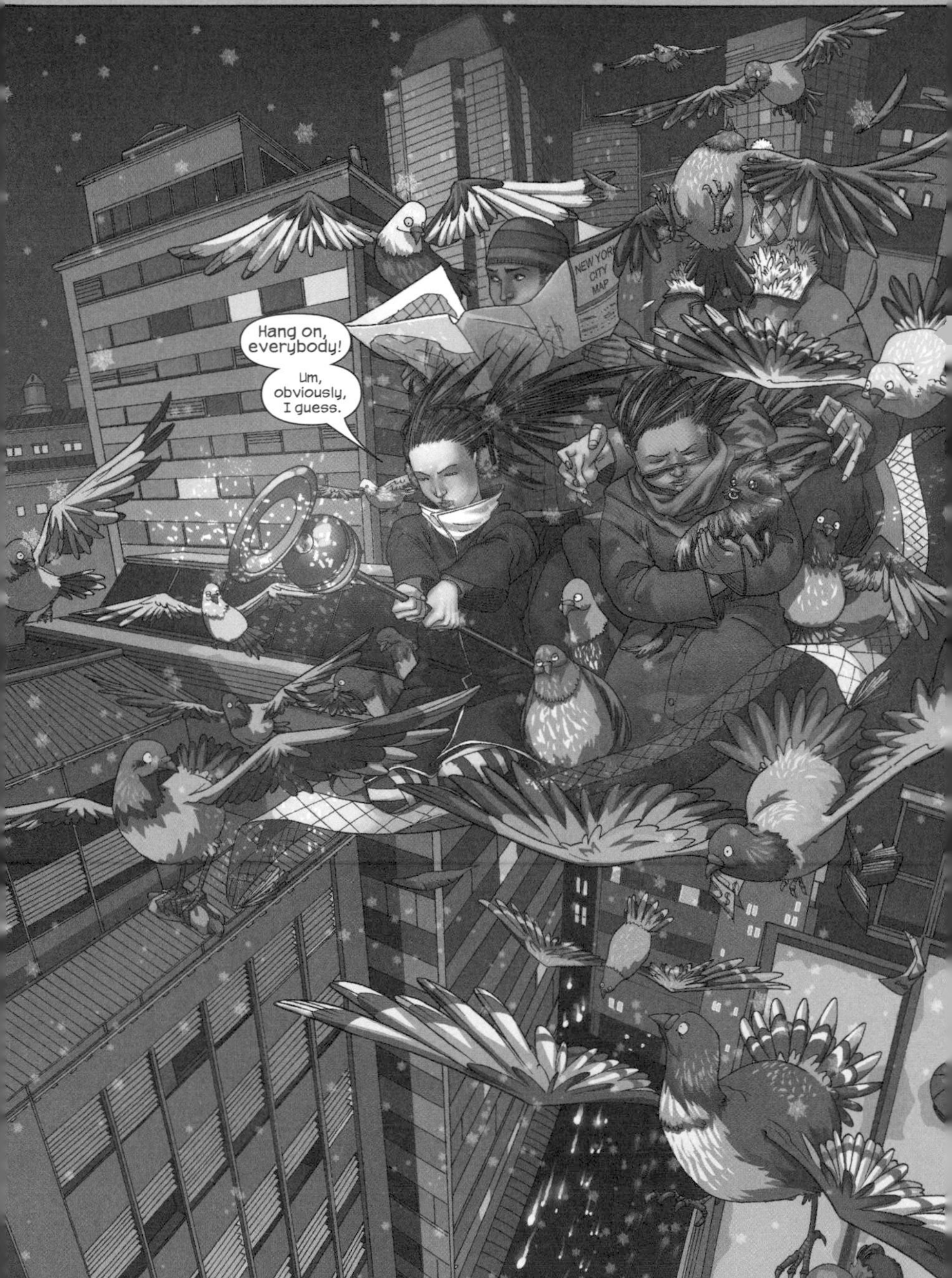
Hang on, everybody!
Um, obviously, I guess.
NEW YORK CITY MAP

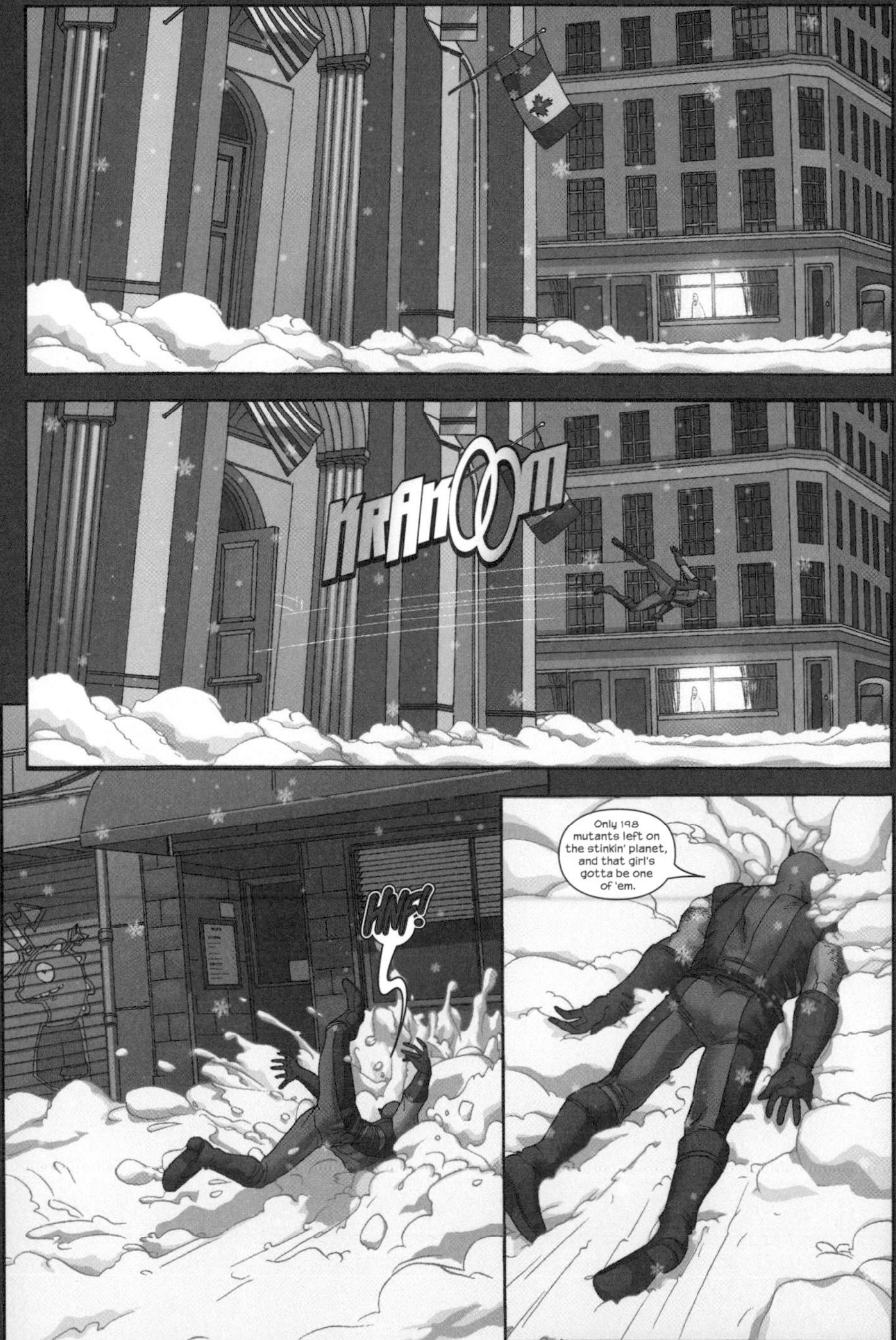
KRAKOOM
HNF!
Only 198 mutants left on the stinkin' planet, and that girl's gotta be one of 'em.

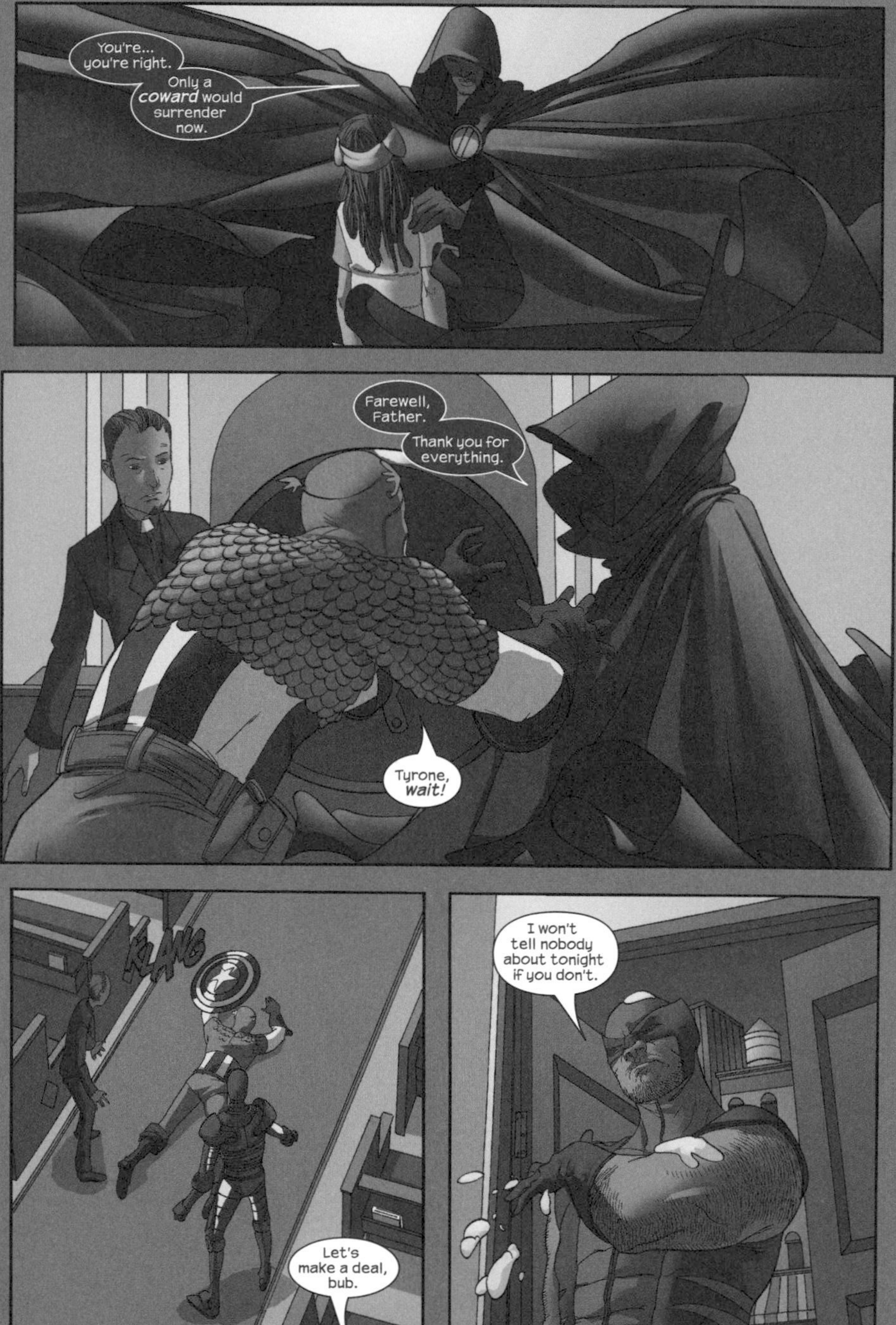

You're... you're right.
Only a *coward* would surrender now.
Farewell, Father.
Thank you for everything.
Tyrone, *wait!*
KLANG
Let's make a deal, bub.
I won't tell nobody about tonight if you don't.

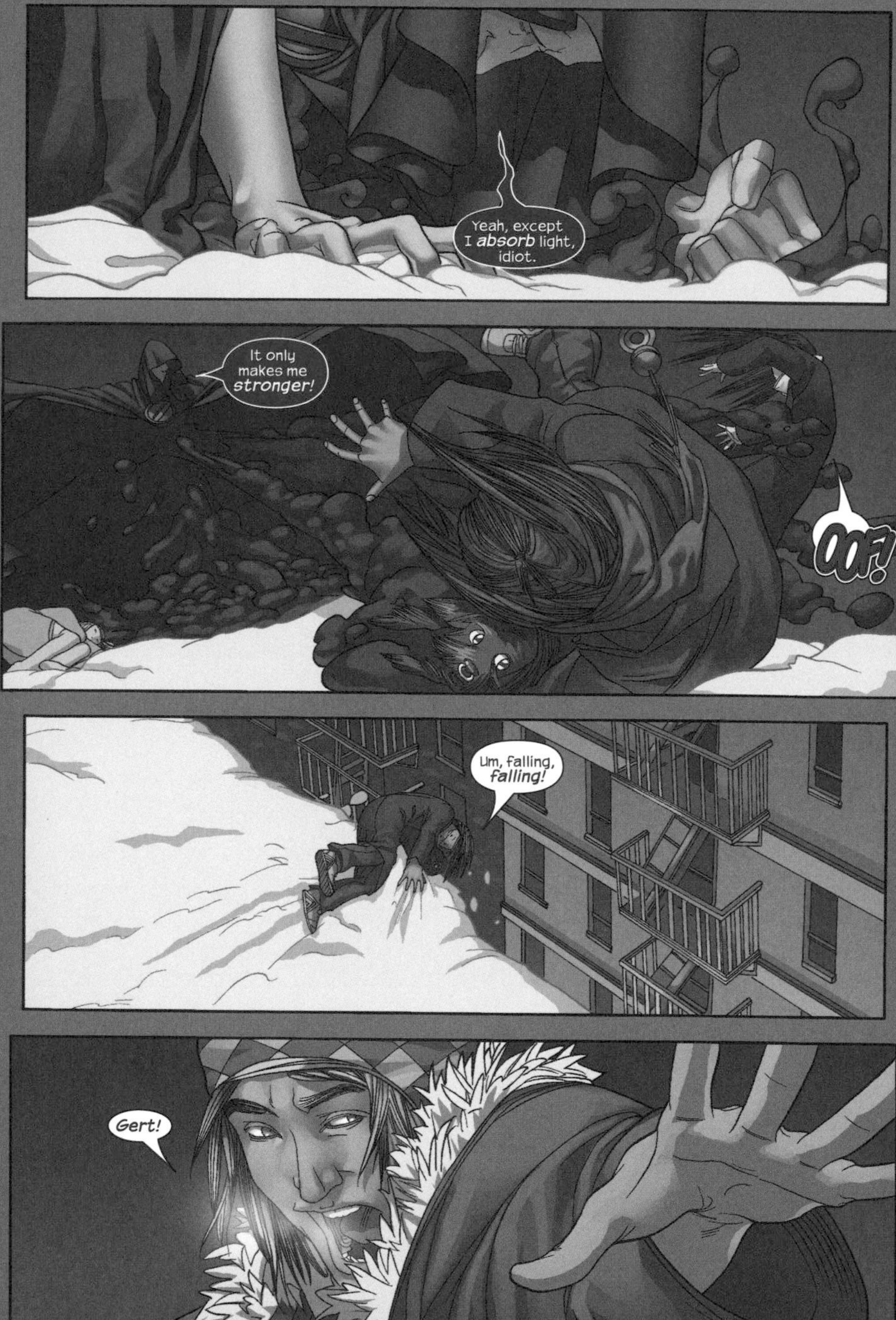
Yeah, except I absorb light, idiot.
It only makes me stronger!
OOF!
Um, falling, falling!
Gert!

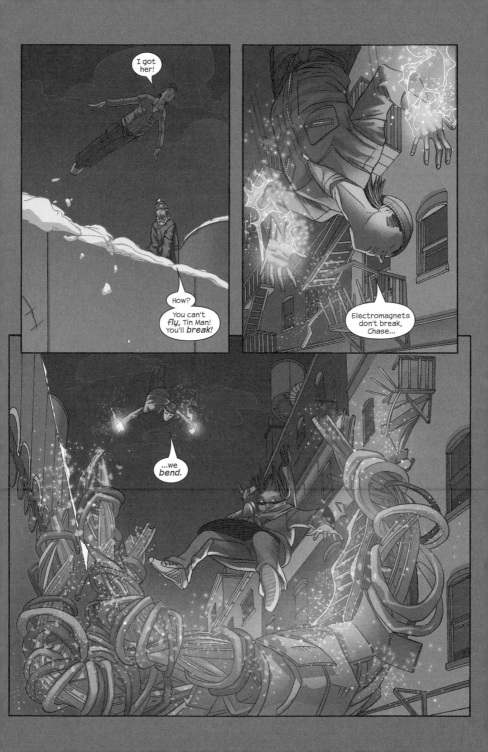

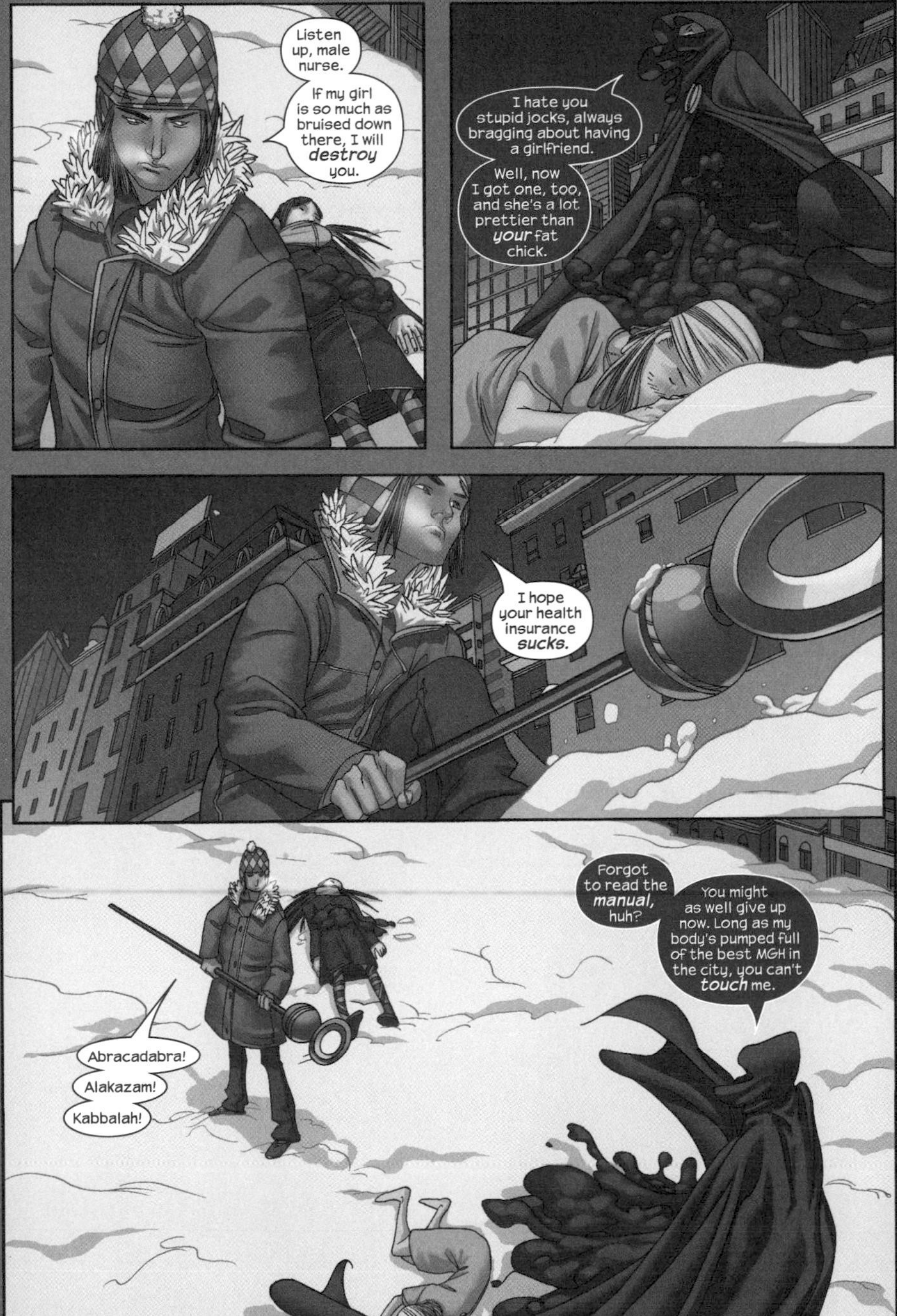
Listen up, male nurse.
If my girl is so much as bruised down there, I will *destroy* you.
I hate you stupid jocks, always bragging about having a girlfriend.
Well, now I got one, too, and she's a lot prettier than *your* fat chick.
I hope your health insurance *sucks.*
Forgot to read the *manual,* huh?
You might as well give up now. Long as my body's pumped full of the best MGH in the city, you can't *touch* me.
Abracadabra!
Alakazam!
Kabbalah!

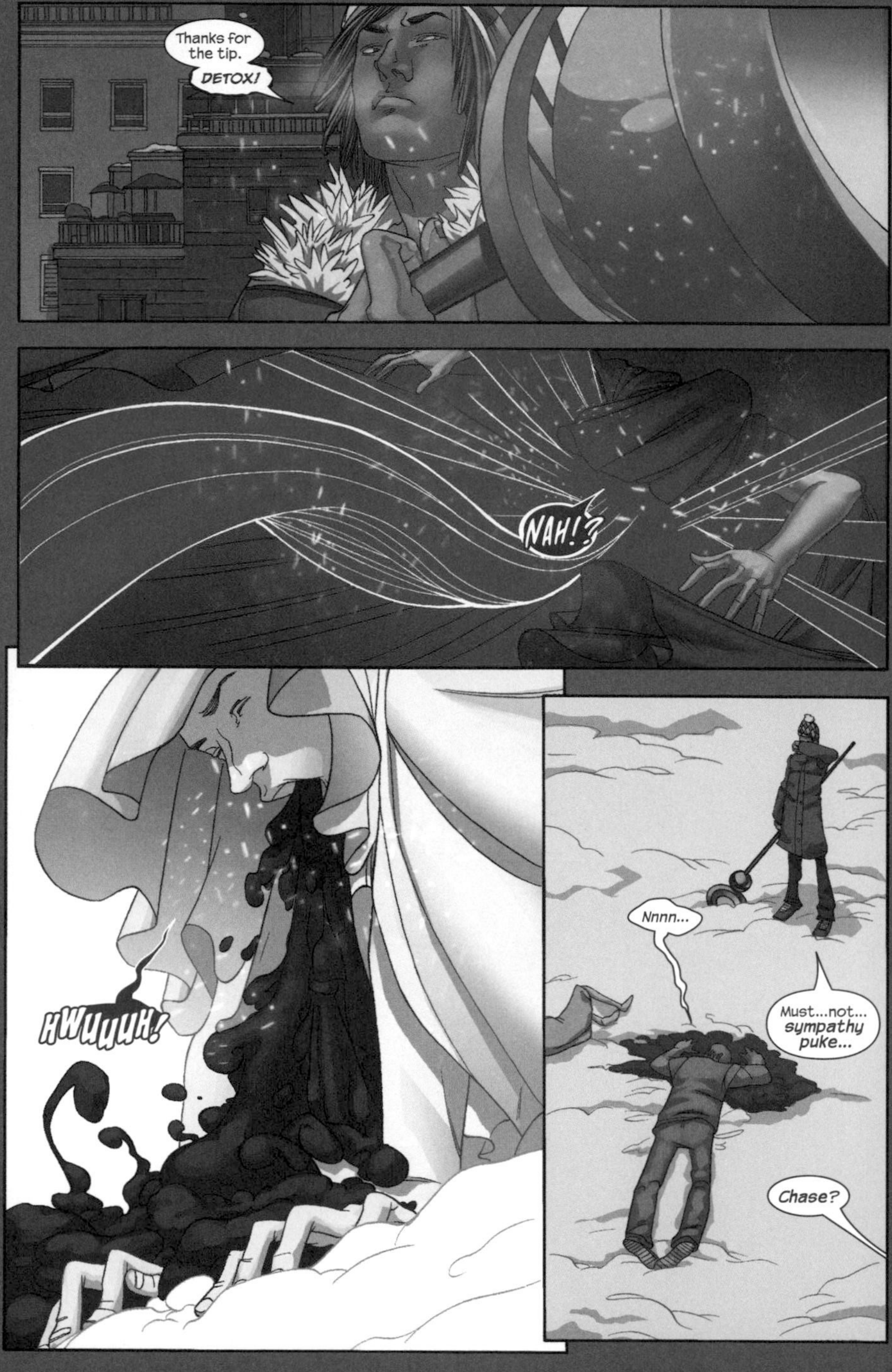
Thanks for the tip.
DETOX!
NAH!?
HWUUUUH!
Nnnn...
Must...not... sympathy puke...
Chase?

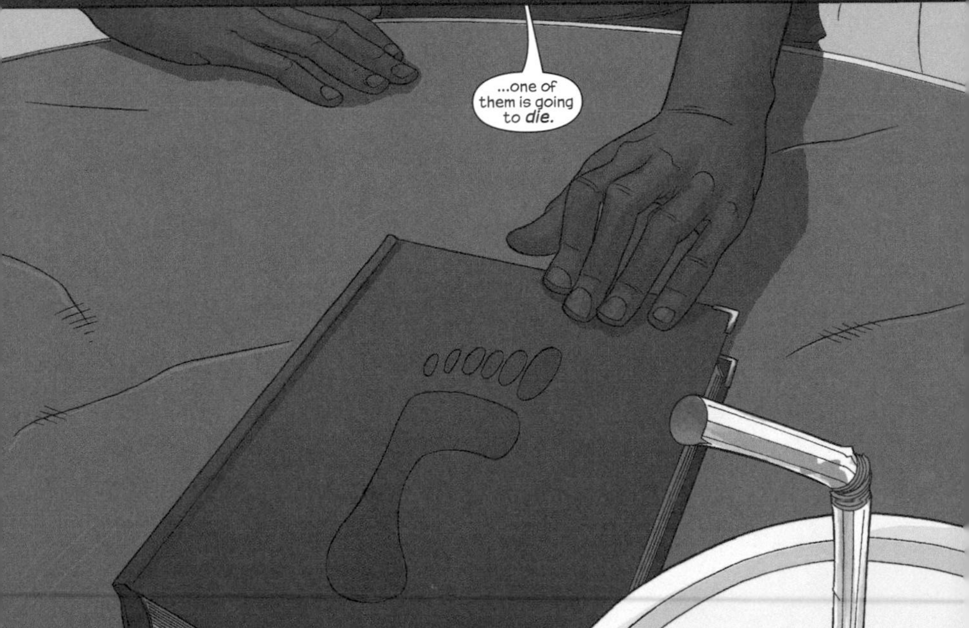
...one of them is going to *die.*

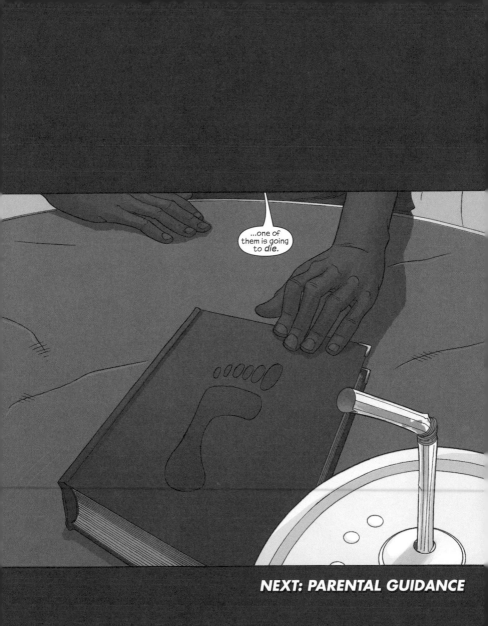

NEXT: PARENTAL GUIDANCE

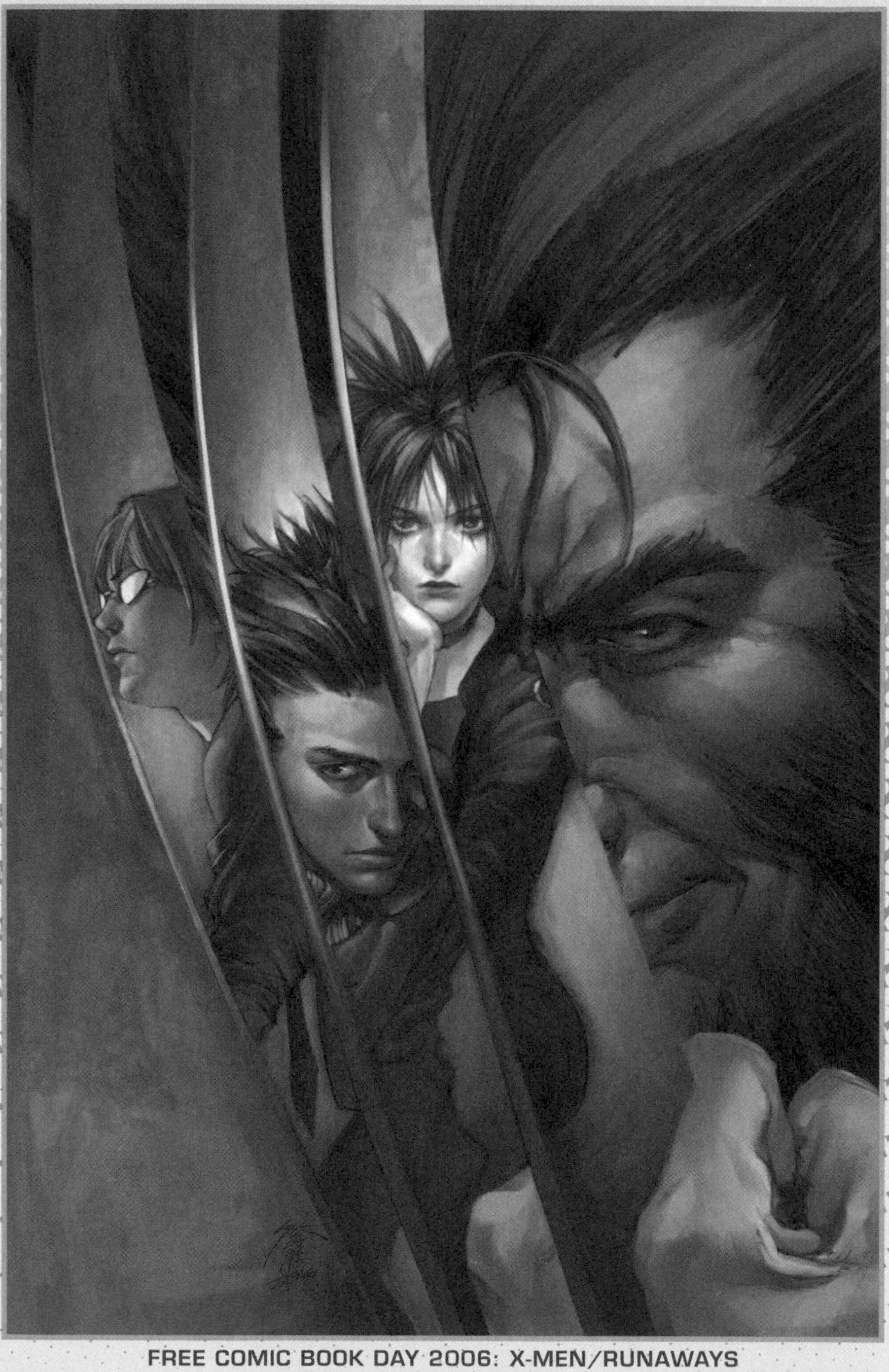

FREE COMIC BOOK DAY 2006: X-MEN/RUNAWAYS

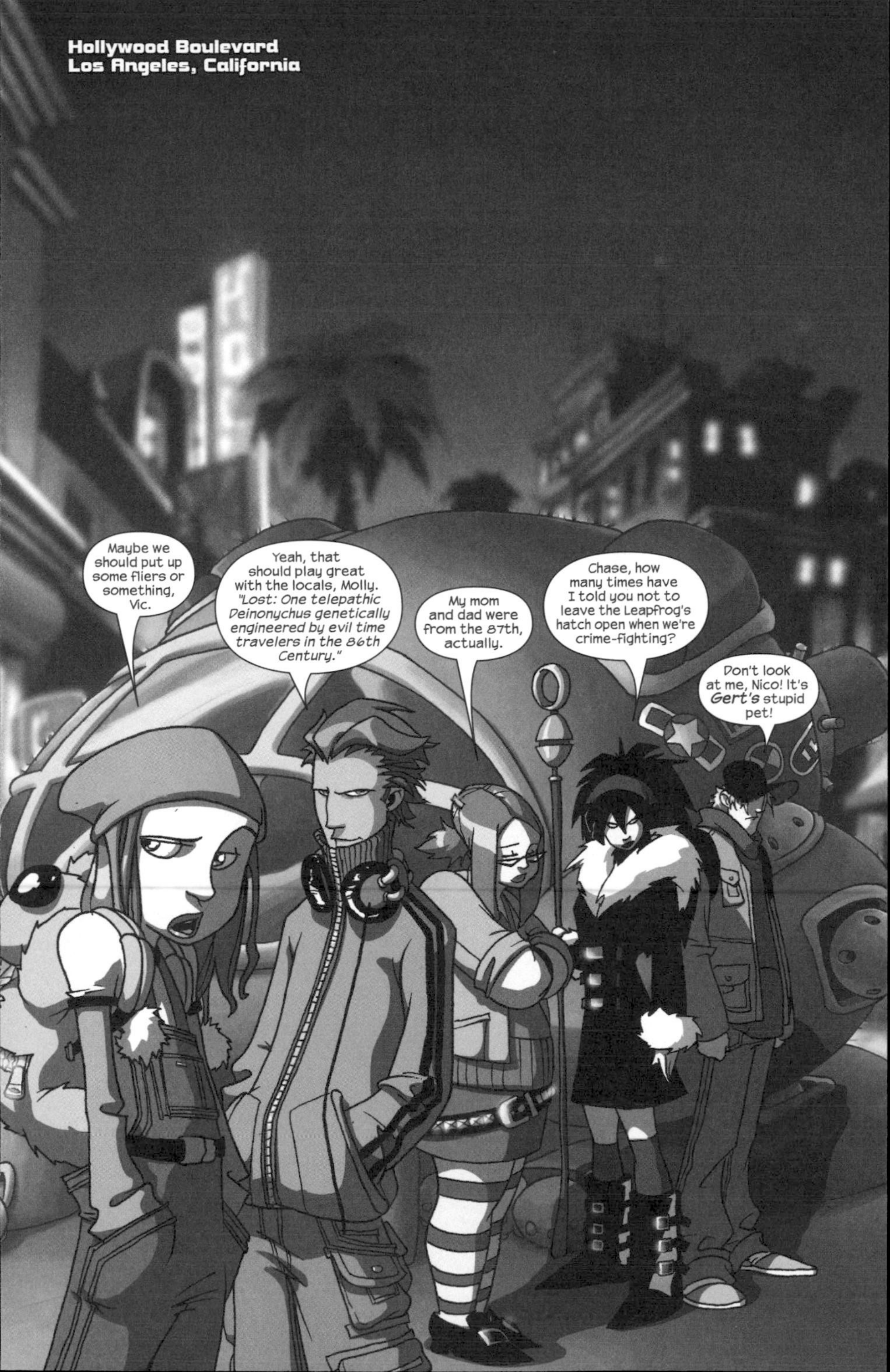
Hollywood Boulevard
Los Angeles, California
Maybe we should put up some fliers or something, Vic.
Yeah, that should play great with the locals, Molly. "Lost: One telepathic Deinonychus genetically engineered by evil time travelers in the 86th Century."
My mom and dad were from the 87th, actually.
Chase, how many times have I told you not to leave the Leapfrog's hatch open when we're crime-fighting?
Don't look at me, Nico! It's Gert's stupid pet!

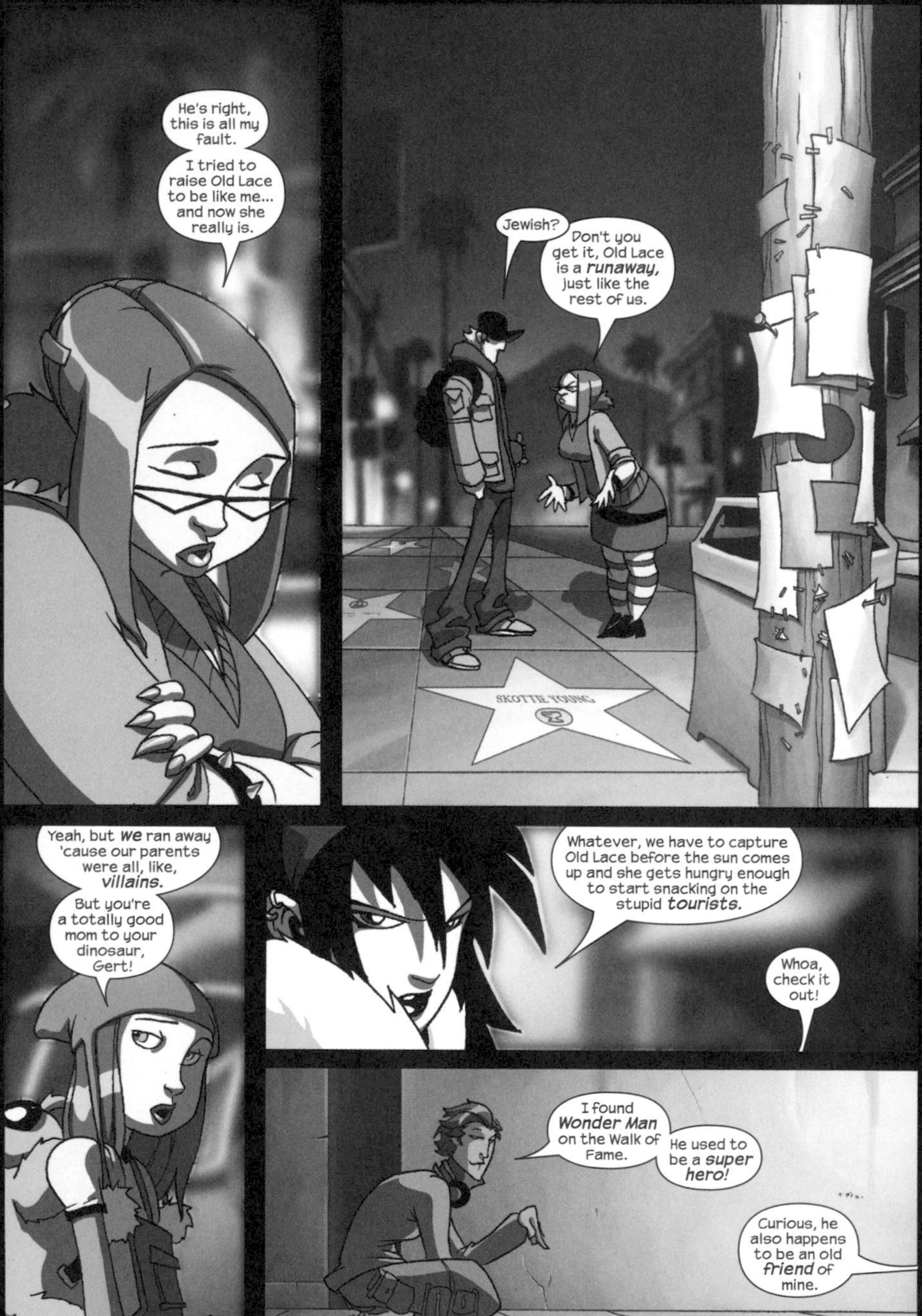
He's right, this is all my fault.
I tried to raise Old Lace to be like me... and now she really is.
Jewish?
Don't you get it, Old Lace is a *runaway,* just like the rest of us.
SKOTTIE YOUNG
Yeah, but *we* ran away 'cause our parents were all, like, *villains.*
But you're a totally good mom to your dinosaur, Gert!
Whatever, we have to capture Old Lace before the sun comes up and she gets hungry enough to start snacking on the stupid *tourists.*
Whoa, check it out!
I found *Wonder Man* on the Walk of Fame.
He used to be a *super hero!*
Curious, he also happens to be an old *friend* of mine.

FREE

BRIAN K. VAUGHAN	SKOTTIE YOUNG	VC'S RANDY GENTILE	JO CHEN	C.B. CEBULSKI	NATHAN COSBY	MACKENZIE CADENHEAD	JOE QUESADA	DAN BUCKLEY
WRITER	ARTIST	LETTERS	COVER ARTIST	SPECIAL THANKS	ASSISTANT EDITOR	EDITOR	EDITOR IN CHIEF	PUBLISHER

RUNAWAYS CREATED BY **BRIAN K. VAUGHAN** AND **ADRIAN ALPHONA**

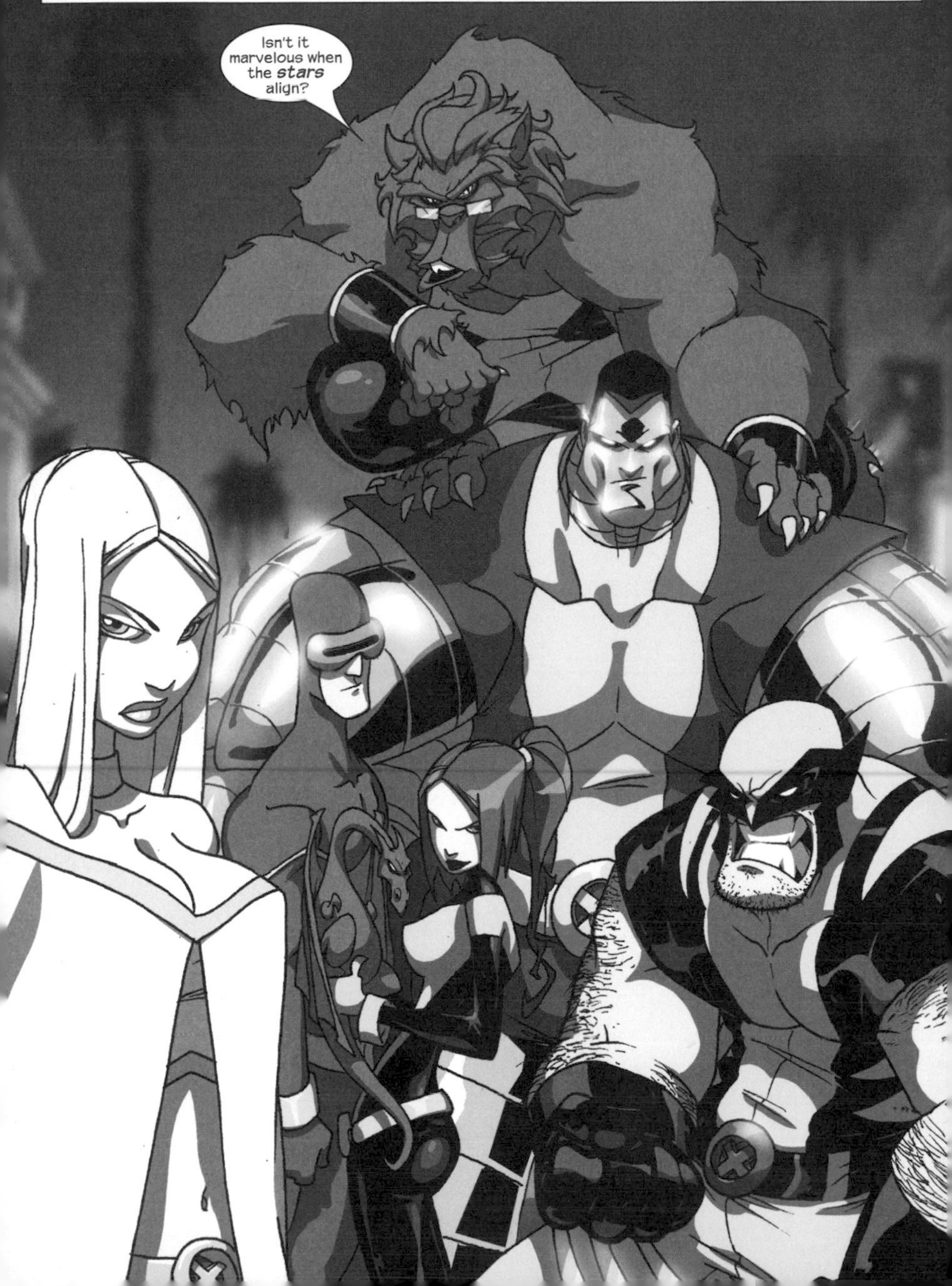

Isn't it marvelous when the *stars* align?

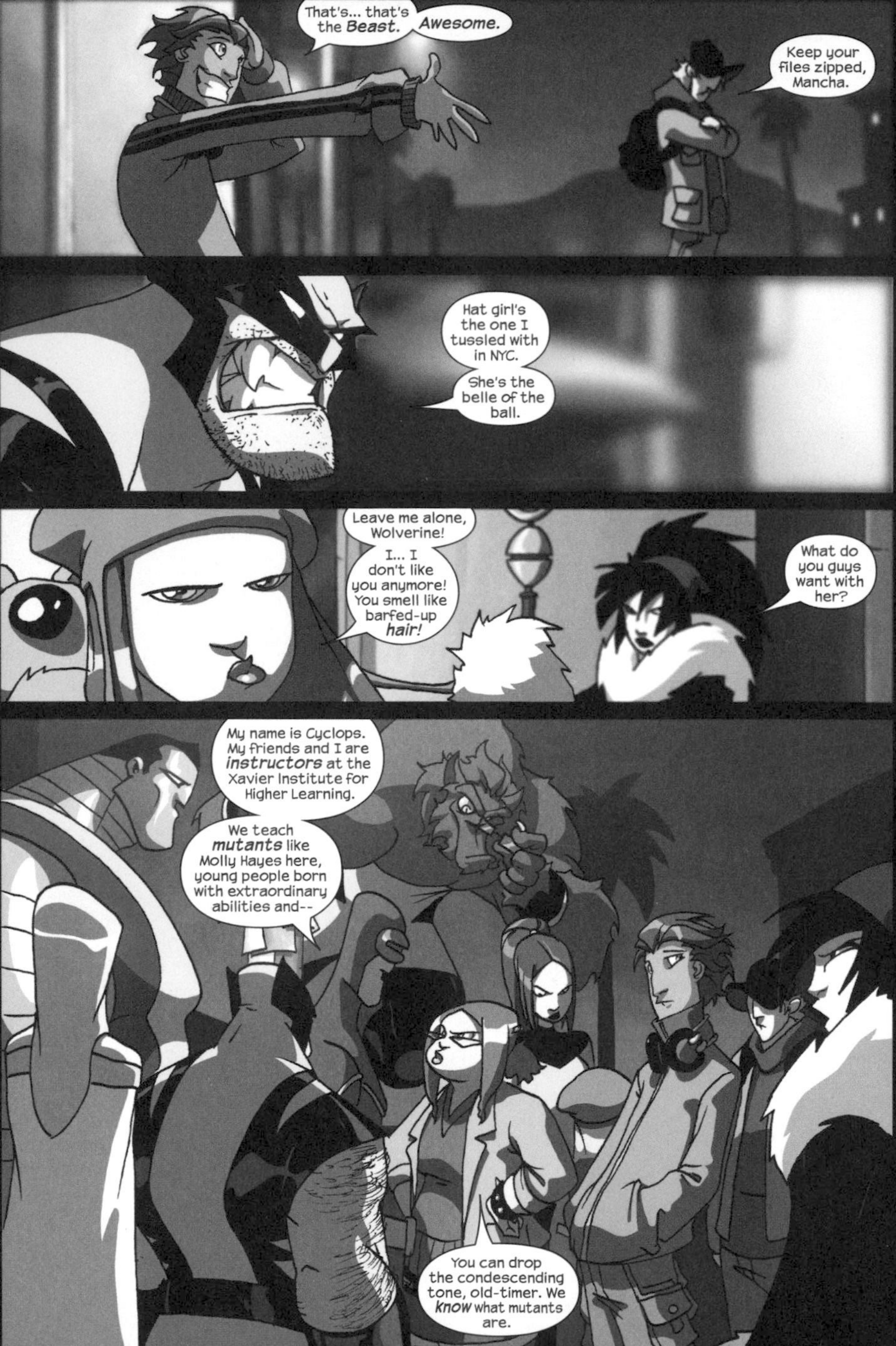
That's... that's the *Beast.*
Awesome.
Keep your files zipped, Mancha.
Hat girl's the one I tussled with in NYC.
She's the belle of the ball.
Leave me alone, Wolverine!
I... I don't like you anymore! You smell like barfed-up *hair!*
What do you guys want with her?
My name is Cyclops. My friends and I are *instructors* at the Xavier Institute for Higher Learning.
We teach *mutants* like Molly Hayes here, young people born with extraordinary abilities and--
You can drop the condescending tone, old-timer. We *know* what mutants are.

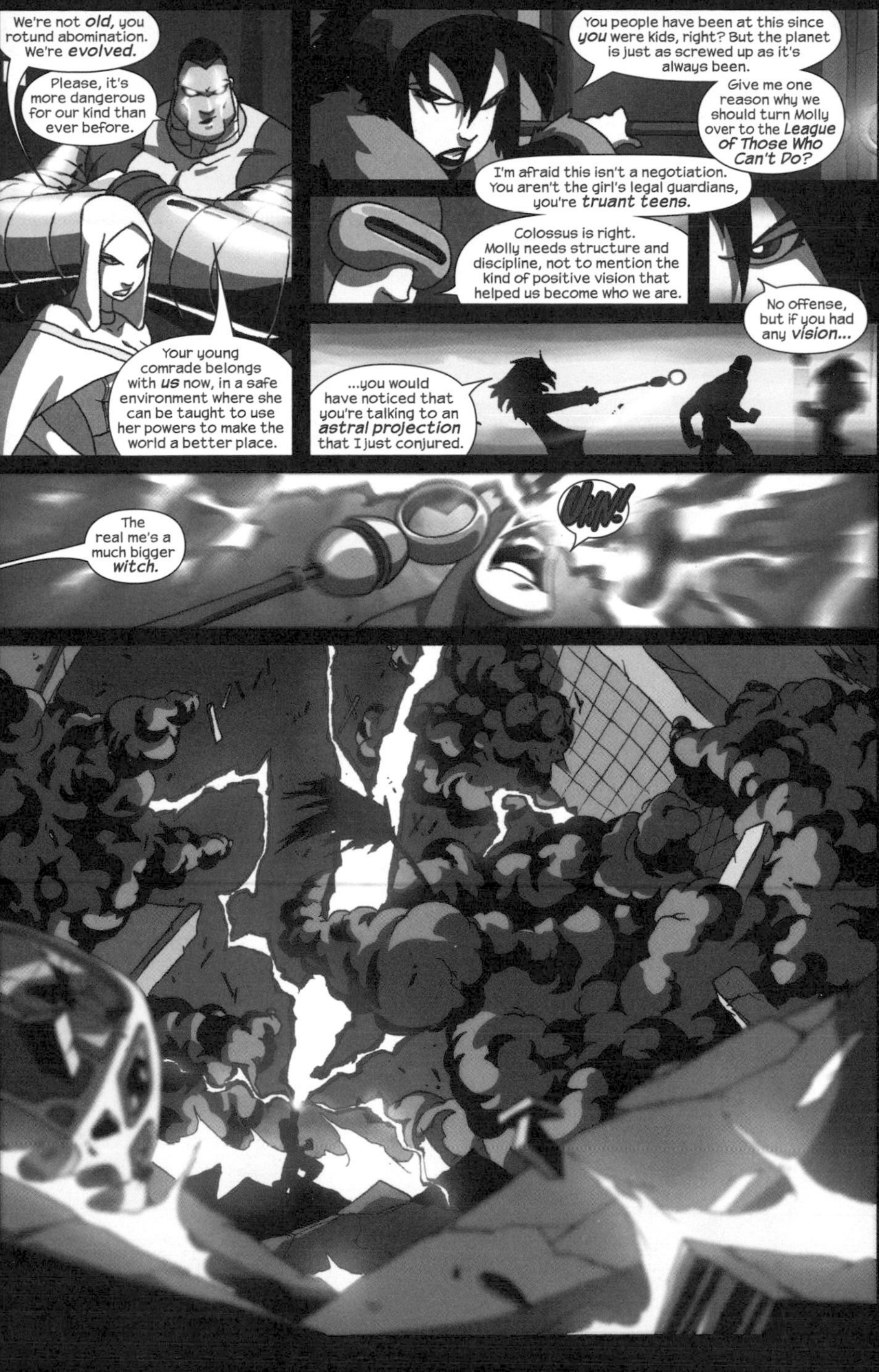

We're not *old,* you rotund abomination. We're *evolved.*
Please, it's more dangerous for our kind than ever before.
Your young comrade belongs with *us* now, in a safe environment where she can be taught to use her powers to make the world a better place.
You people have been at this since *you* were kids, right? But the planet is just as screwed up as it's always been.
Give me one reason why we should turn Molly over to the *League of Those Who Can't Do?*
I'm afraid this isn't a negotiation. You aren't the girl's legal guardians, you're *truant teens.*
Colossus is right. Molly needs structure and discipline, not to mention the kind of positive vision that helped us become who we are.
No offense, but if you had any *vision...*
...you would have noticed that you're talking to an *astral projection* that I just conjured.
The real me's a much bigger *witch.*

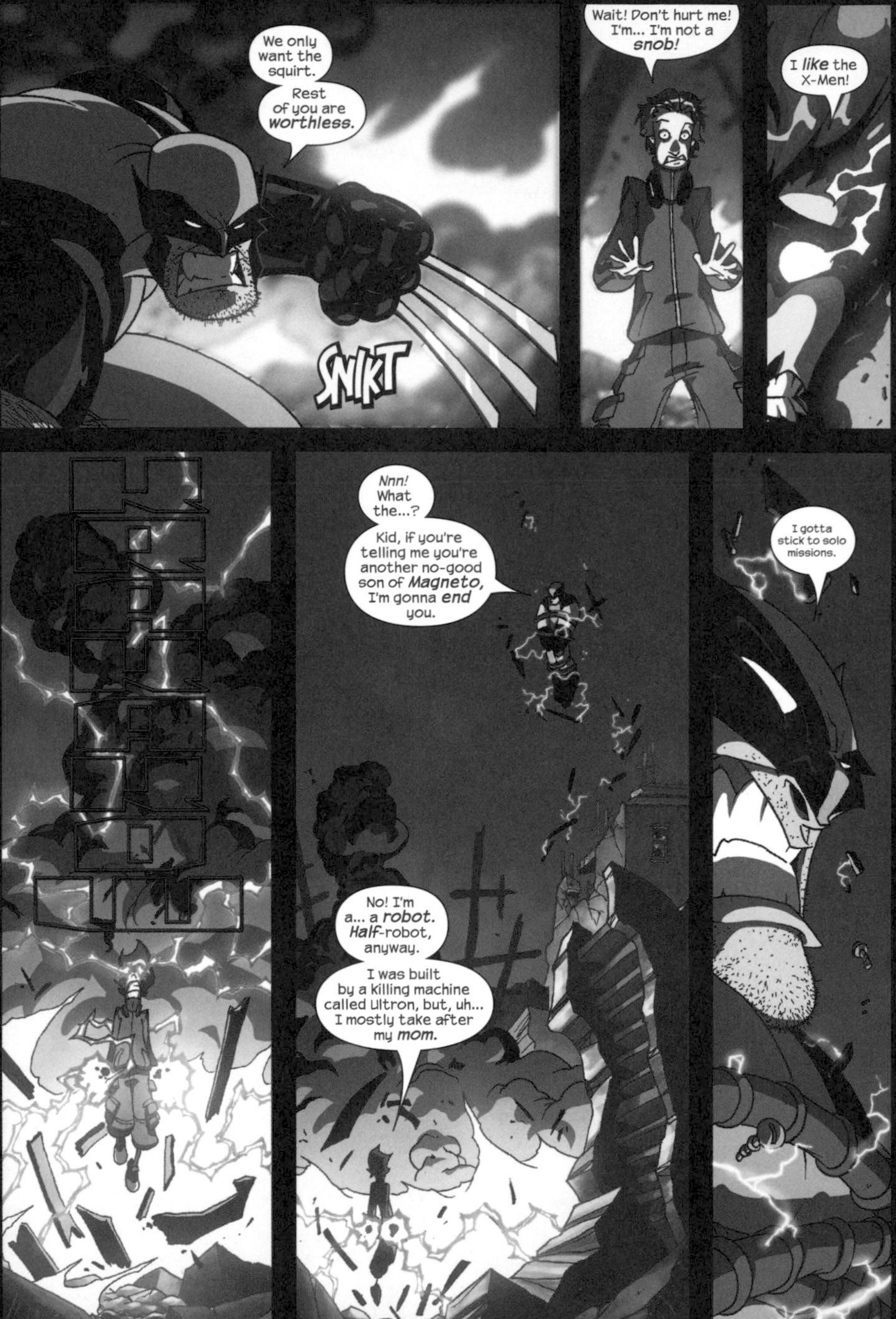
We only want the squirt.
Rest of you are worthless.
SNIKT
Wait! Don't hurt me! I'm... I'm not a snob!
I like the X-Men!
Nnn! What the...?
Kid, if you're telling me you're another no-good son of Magneto, I'm gonna end you.
No! I'm a... a robot. Half-robot, anyway.
I was built by a killing machine called Ultron, but, uh... I mostly take after my mom.
I gotta stick to solo missions.

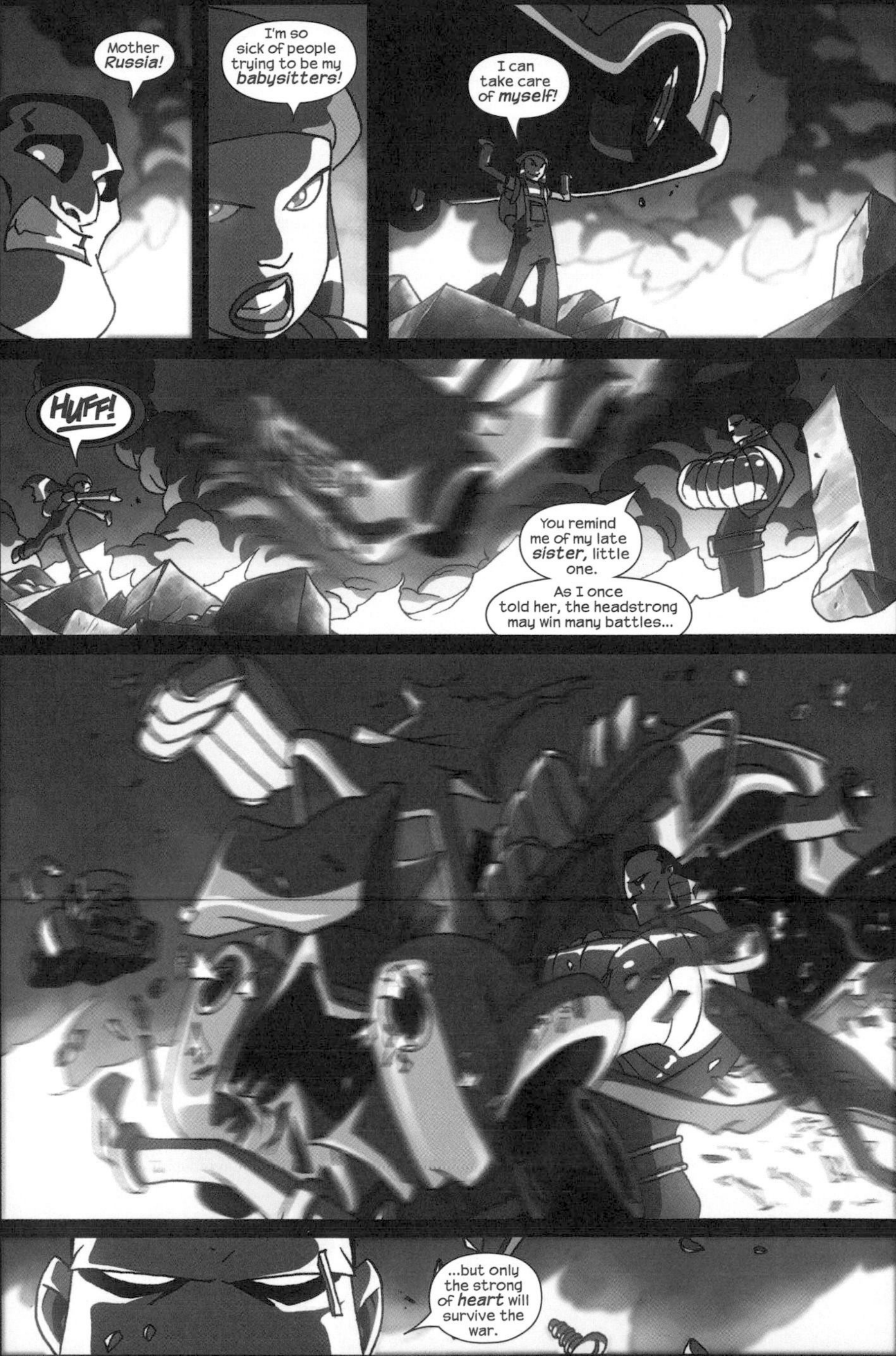
Mother Russia!
I'm so sick of people trying to be my babysitters!
I can take care of myself!
HUFF!
You remind me of my late sister, little one.
As I once told her, the headstrong may win many battles...
...but only the strong of heart will survive the war.

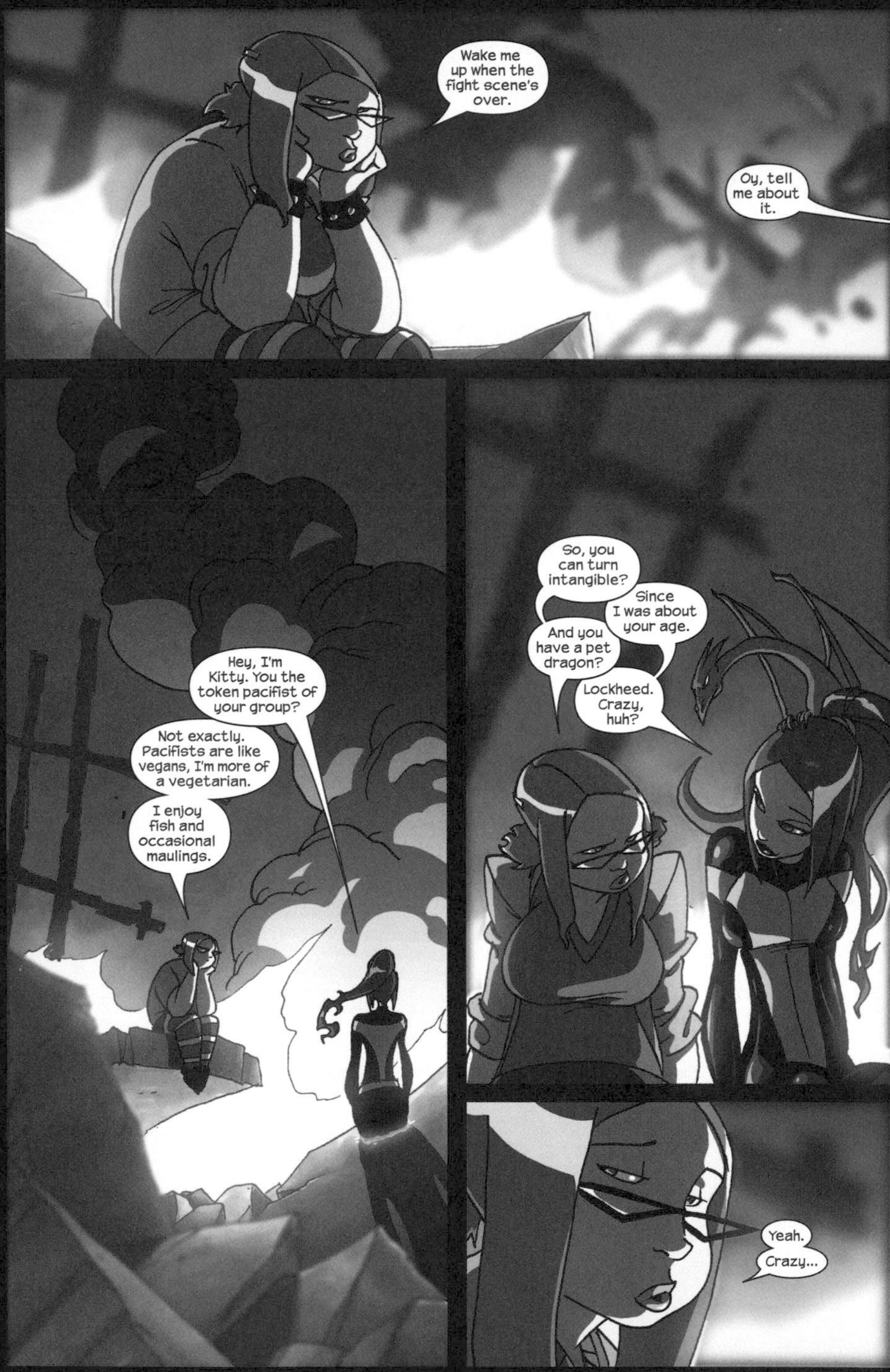
Wake me up when the fight scene's over.
Oy, tell me about it.
Hey, I'm Kitty. You the token pacifist of your group?
Not exactly. Pacifists are like vegans, I'm more of a vegetarian.
I enjoy fish and occasional maulings.
So, you can turn intangible?
Since I was about your age.
And you have a pet dragon?
Lockheed. Crazy, huh?
Yeah.
Crazy...

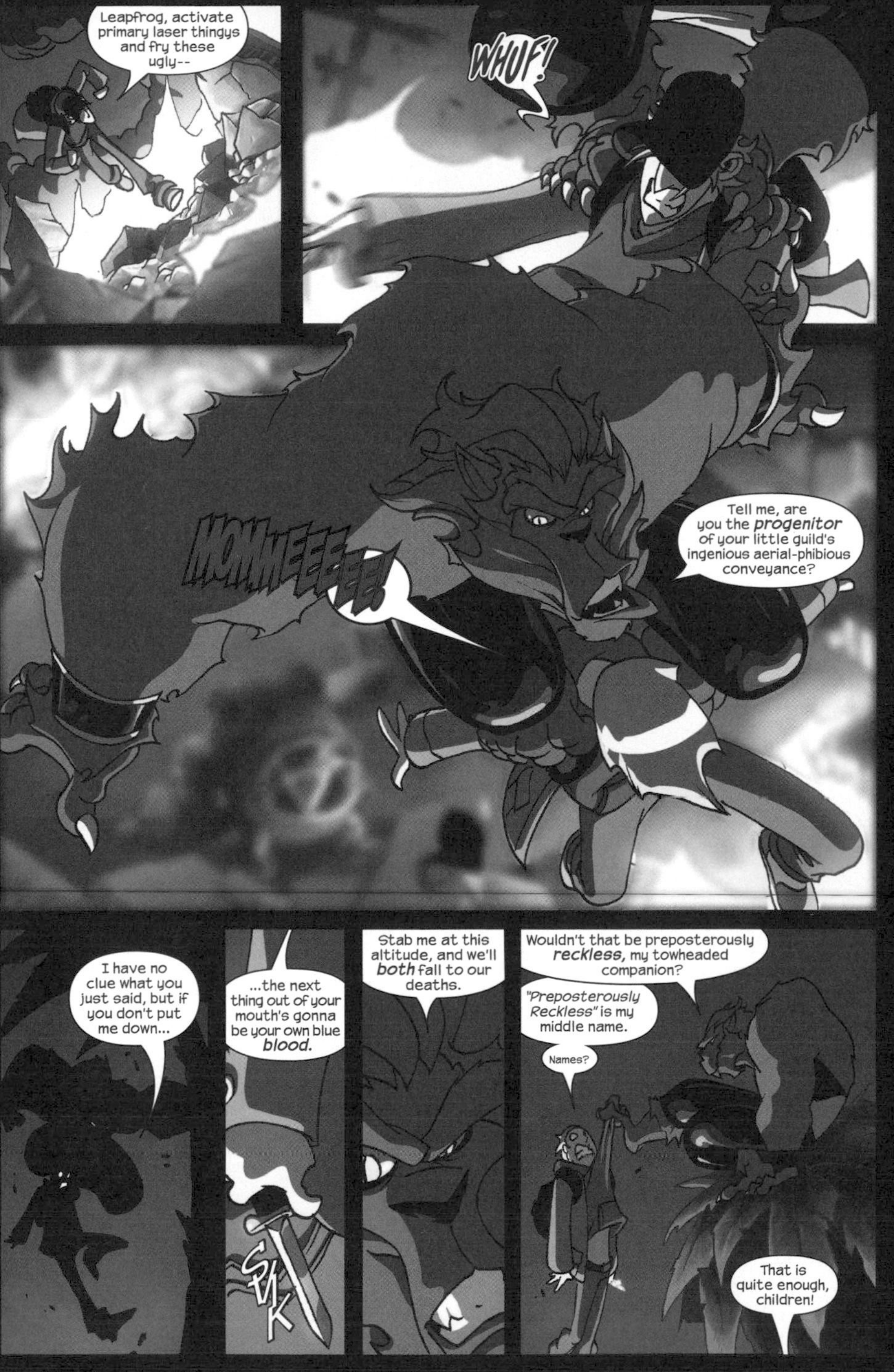
Leapfrog, activate primary laser thingys and fry these ugly--
WHUF!
MOMMEEEEEE!
Tell me, are you the *progenitor* of your little guild's ingenious aerial-phibious conveyance?
I have no clue what you just said, but if you don't put me down...
...the next thing out of your mouth's gonna be your own blue *blood.*
SNIK
Stab me at this altitude, and we'll *both* fall to our deaths.
Wouldn't that be preposterously *reckless,* my towheaded companion?
"Preposterously Reckless" is my middle name.
Names?
That is quite enough, children!

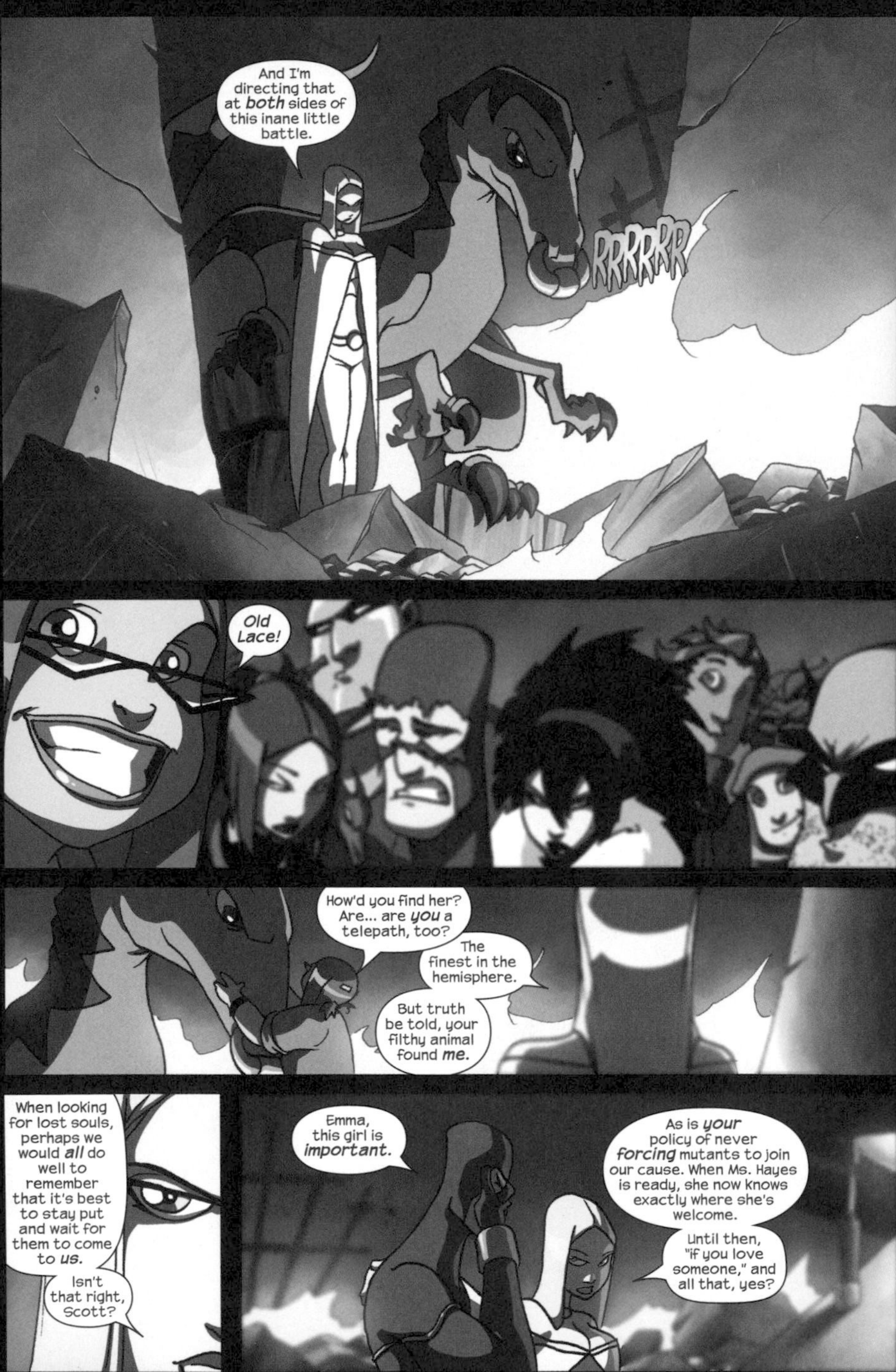
And I'm directing that at *both* sides of this inane little battle.
RRRRRR
Old Lace!
How'd you find her? Are... are *you* a telepath, too?
The finest in the hemisphere.
But truth be told, your filthy animal found *me*.
When looking for lost souls, perhaps we would *all* do well to remember that it's best to stay put and wait for them to come to *us*.
Isn't that right, Scott?
Emma, this girl is *important*.
As is *your* policy of never *forcing* mutants to join our cause. When Ms. Hayes is ready, she now knows exactly where she's welcome.
Until then, "if you love someone," and all that, yes?

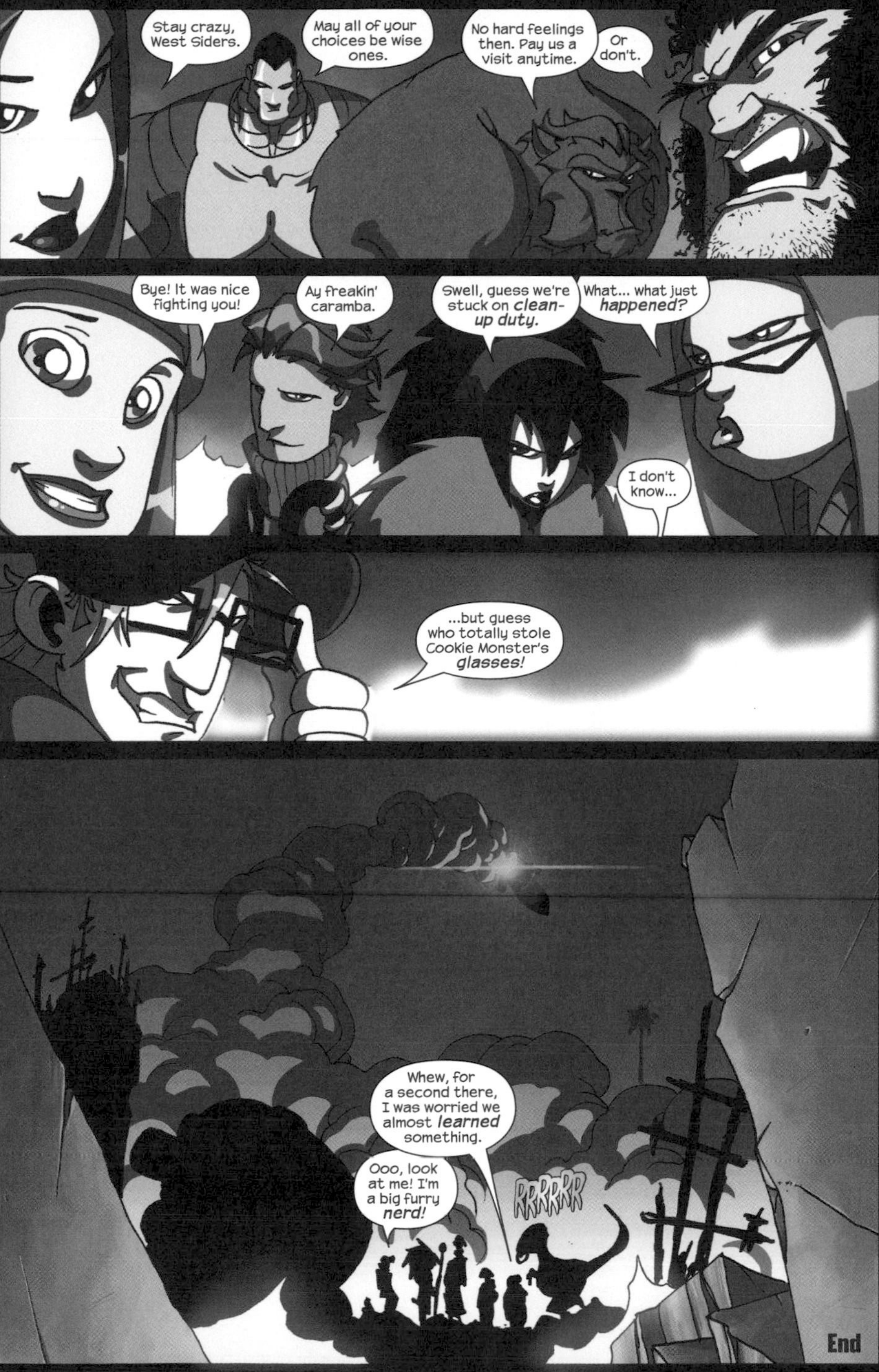
Stay crazy, West Siders.
May all of your choices be wise ones.
No hard feelings then. Pay us a visit anytime.
Or don't.
Bye! It was nice fighting you!
Ay freakin' caramba.
Swell, guess we're stuck on *clean-up duty.*
What... what just *happened?*
I don't know...
...but guess who totally stole Cookie Monster's *glasses!*
Whew, for a second there, I was worried we almost *learned* something.
Ooo, look at me! I'm a big furry *nerd!*
RRRRRR
End

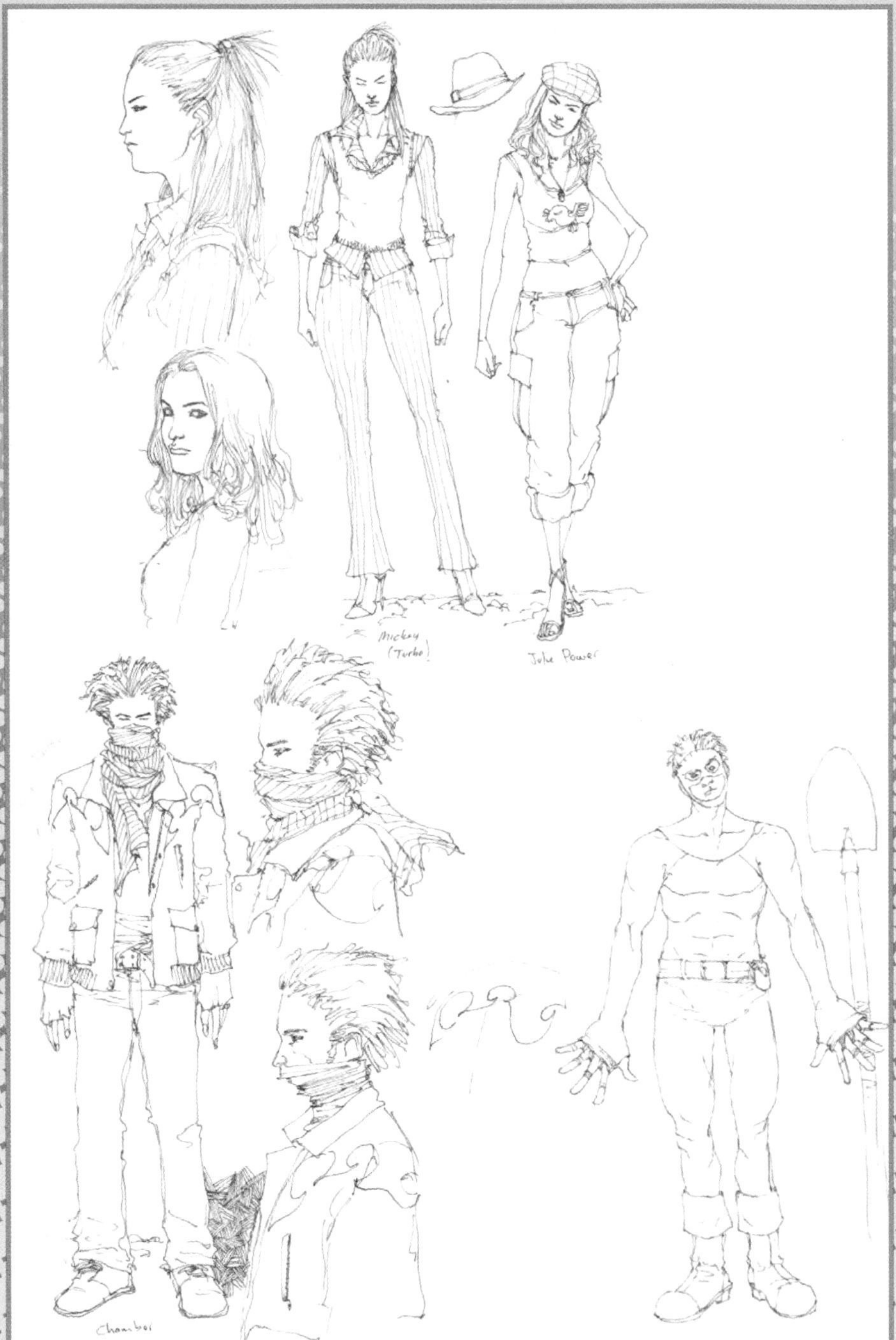
Mickey
(Turbo)
Julie Power
Chamber

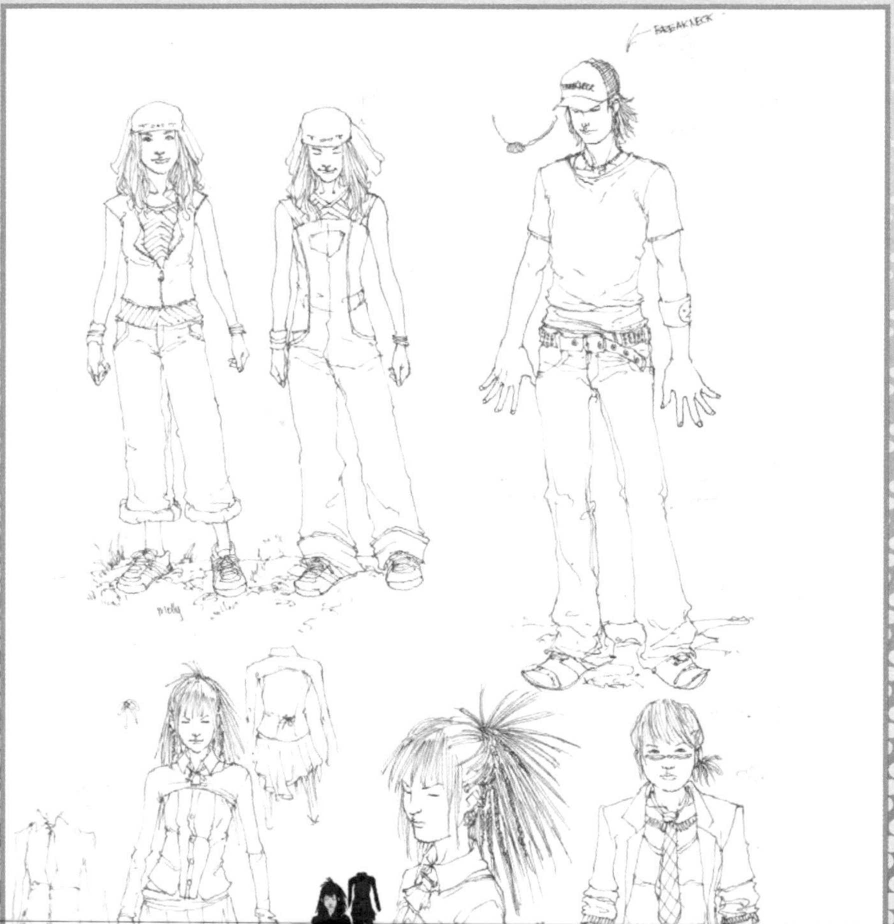
BREAKNECK
molly
nico
Gert

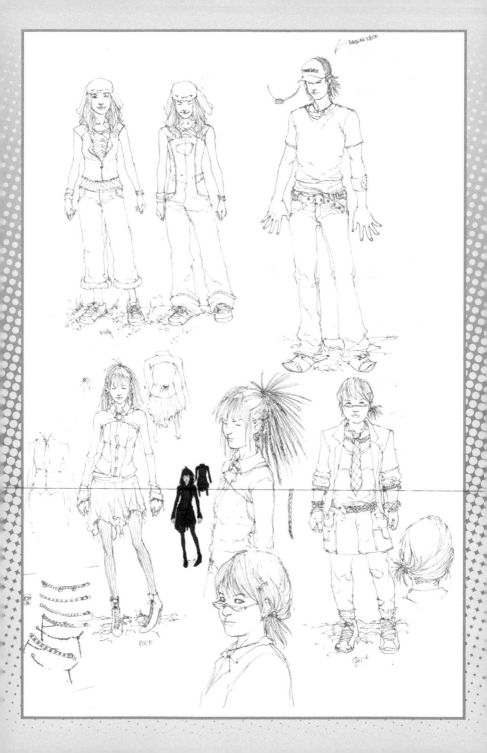

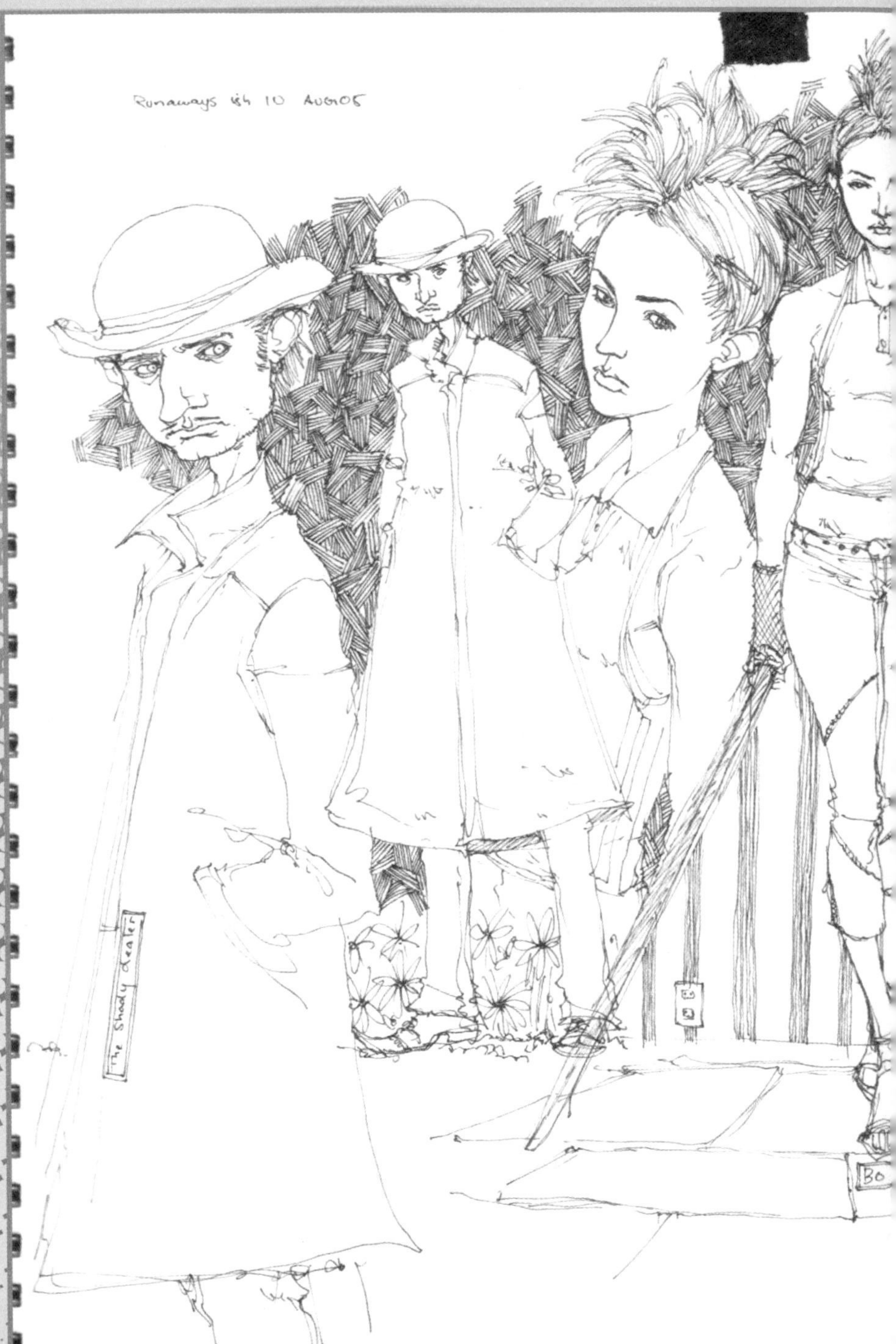
Runaways ish 10 AUG05
The Shady dealer
BO

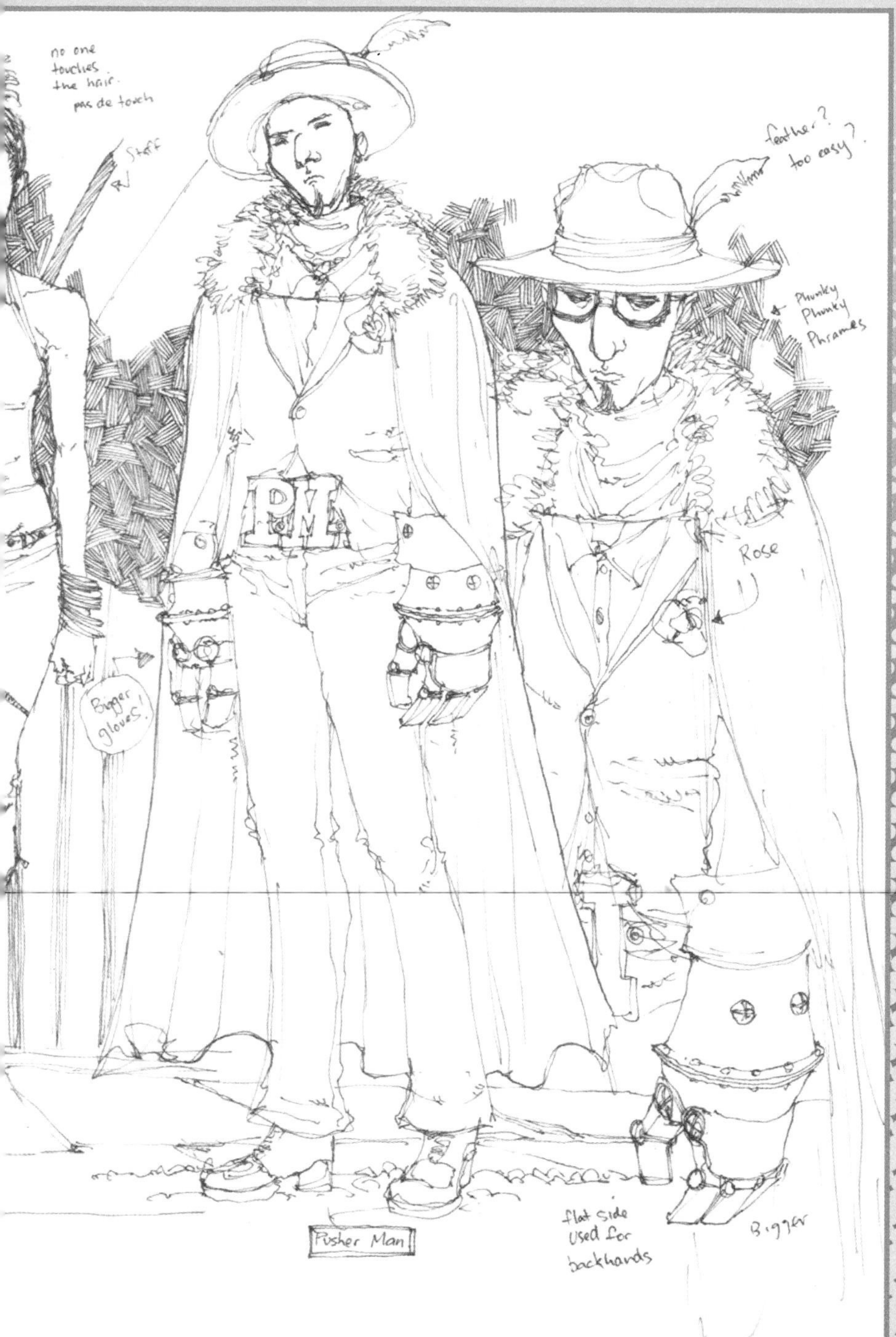
no one
touches
the hair.
pas de touch
Staff
feather?
too easy?
Phunky
Phunky
Phrames
Rose
Bigger
gloves!
Pusher Man
flat side
used for
backhands
Bigger

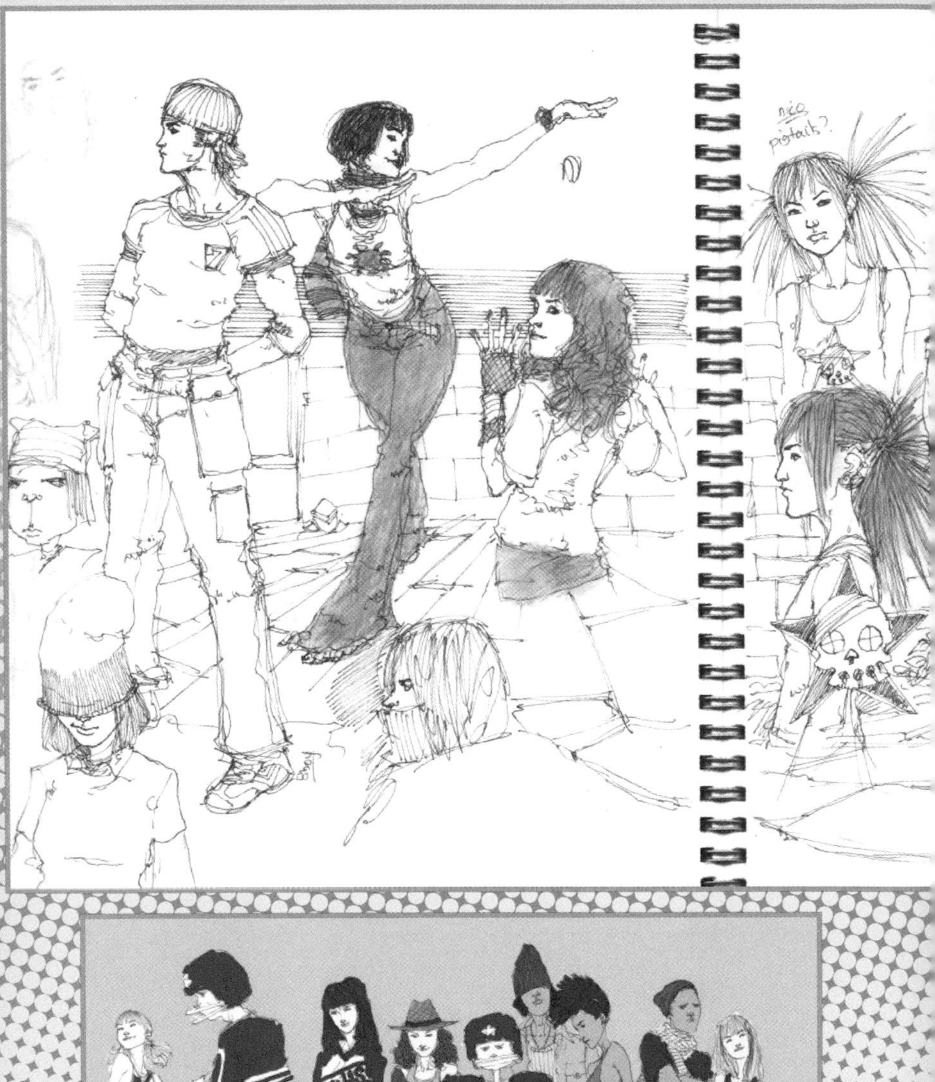
nico
pigtails?

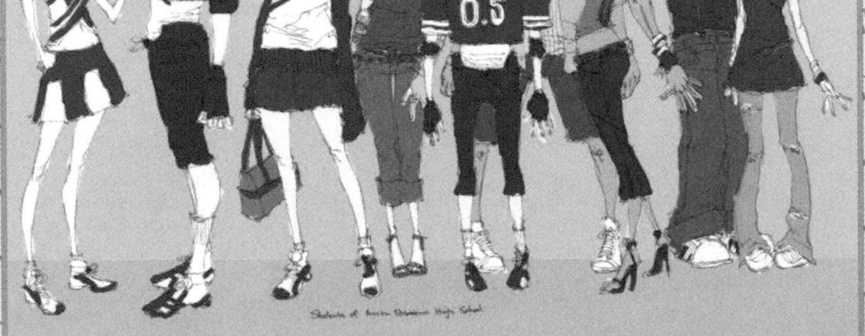
APHS
0.5

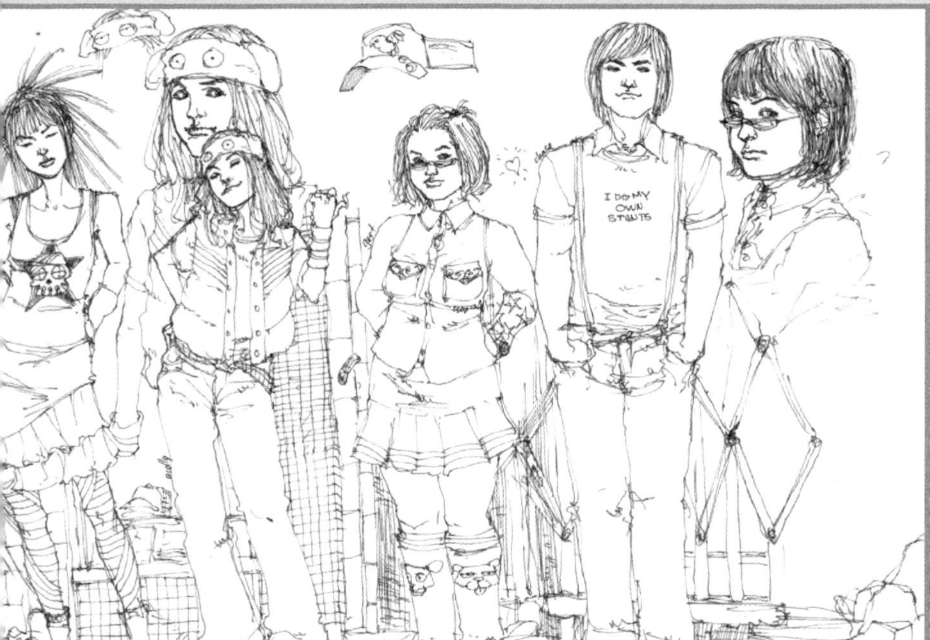
I DO MY OWN STUNTS
Runaways for issue 9!

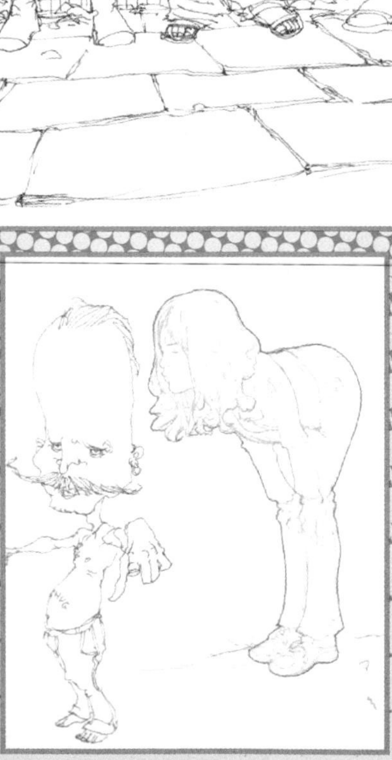

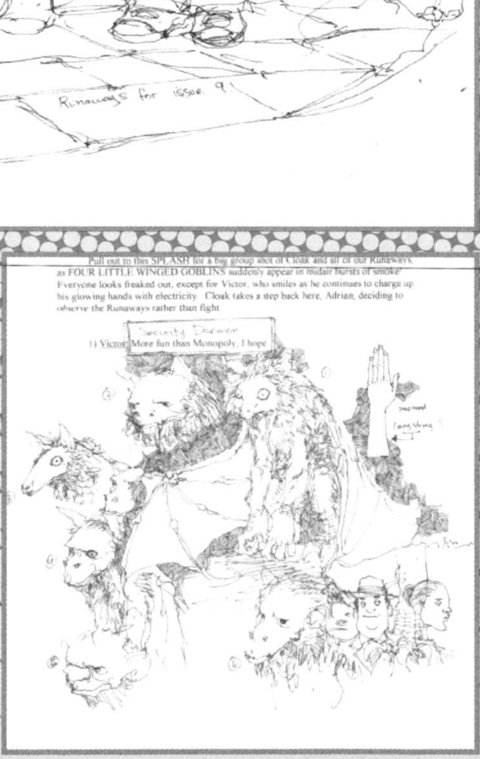
Pull out to this SPLASH for a big group shot of Cloak and all of our Runaways, as FOUR LITTLE WINGED GOBLINS suddenly appear in midair bursts of smoke! Everyone looks freaked out, except for Victor, who smiles as he continues to charge up his glowing hands with electricity. Cloak takes a step back here, Adrian, deciding to *observe* the Runaways rather than fight
Security Daemon
1) Victor: More fun than Monopoly, I hope

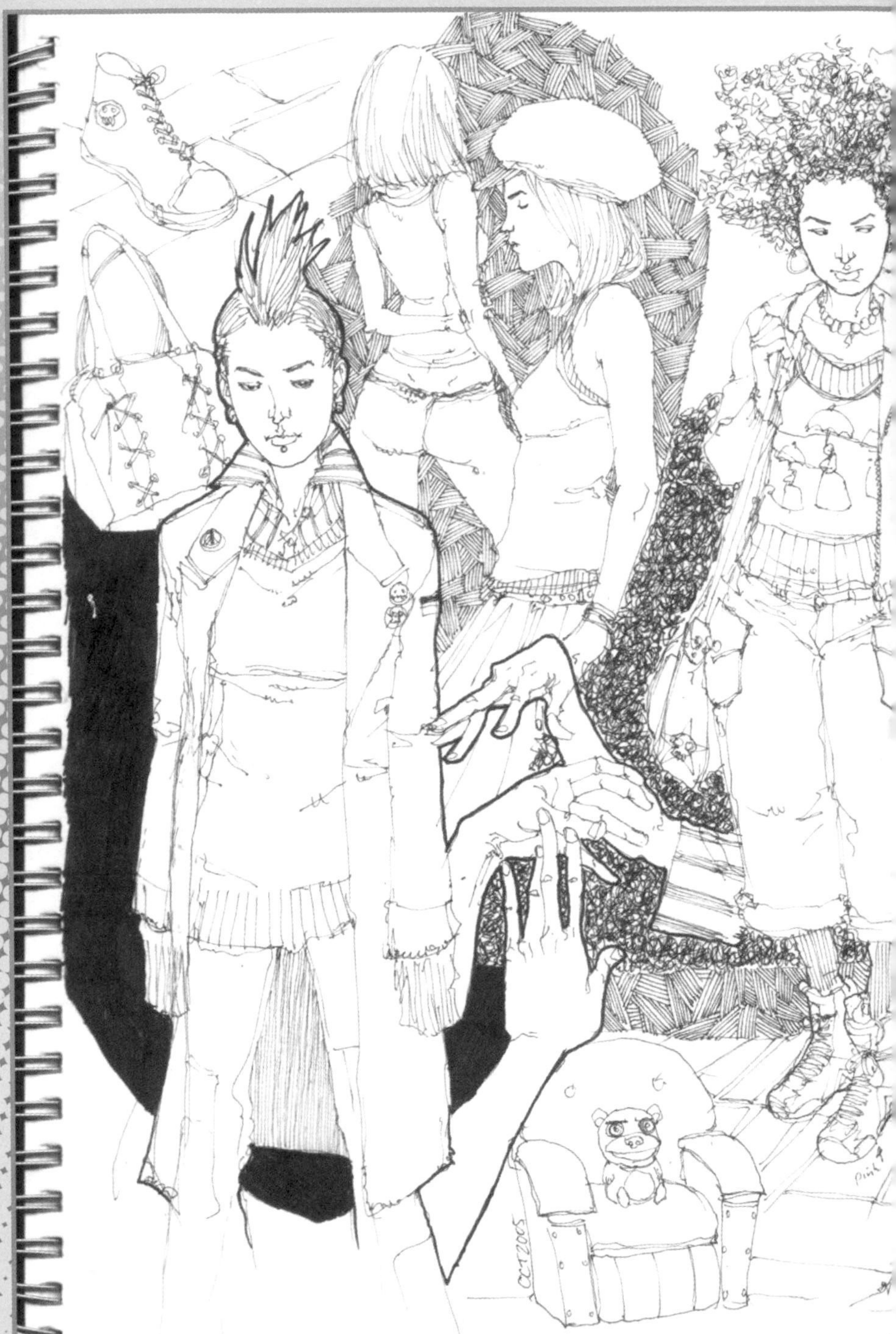
OCT2005